To Katherine,

BRITAIN'S
LANDMARKS
AND
LEGENDS

On the occasion of another
30th Birthday,

Happy Birthday 2024
from Nick

'Places are never just places: they are story and myth and belief.'

(Philip Marsden, *The Summer Isles*, 2019)

BRITAIN'S
LANDMARKS
AND
LEGENDS

The Fascinating Stories
Embedded in Our Landscape

Jo Woolf

Published by National Trust Books
An imprint of HarperCollins Publishers
1 London Bridge Street, London SE1 9GF
www.harpercollins.co.uk

HarperCollins Publishers
Macken House, 39/40 Mayor Street Upper, Dublin 1, D01 C9W8, Ireland

First published 2023

ISBN 978-0-00-856764-4

10 9 8 7 6 5 4 3 2

A catalogue record for this book is available from the British Library.

Printed and bound in Latvia

If you would like to comment on any aspect of this book, please contact us at the above address or
national.trust@harpercollins.co.uk

National Trust publications are available at National Trust shops or online at nationaltrustbooks.co.uk

This book contains FSC™ certified paper and other controlled
sources to ensure responsible forest management.

For more information visit: www.harpercollins.co.uk/green

CONTENTS

INTRODUCTION

In Rudyard Kipling's short story 'Weland's Sword', two children called Dan and Una go out into a meadow on Midsummer's Eve and perform some scenes from *A Midsummer Night's Dream* while standing in a fairy ring. They are just having fun, and their only spectators – or so they think – are three cows grazing by the mill stream. But after their third performance they are astonished to see an elf emerging from the bushes. With a wide grin, he announces himself as Puck of Pook's Hill, and asks them what on earth they think they are doing, re-enacting this play beneath one of the oldest hills in Old England.

> 'By Oak, Ash and Thorn!' he cried, still laughing. 'If this had happened a few hundred years ago you'd have had all the People of the Hills out like bees in June!'
>
> ('Weland's Sword', *Puck of Pook's Hill*, 1906)

Puck tells Dan and Una that they have 'broken the Hills', which hasn't happened for a thousand years. And by 'breaking' the hills, he means the summoning forth of their inhabitants from the spirit realm, with all their attendant powers – a feat which generations of kings, knights and scholars would have given much to accomplish. Perhaps the opening of this unseen door could only have been achieved by children, whose imaginations are untroubled by the need to distinguish fact from fantasy or history from legend.

In the world that Puck describes, it seems as if every feature, whether a hill or a wood or a lake, was once haunted by characters from another realm, and their stories now lie half-forgotten beneath the tramp of human feet. This is Britain's landscape, as it was perceived by our ancestors. In their minds, there was a story embedded in everything, and that story, complete with its giants and monsters and spirit-beings, was an integral part of who they were.

> Through the sand the water slips, and through the mist the light glides away. Nearer comes the formless shadow, and the visible earth grows smaller. The path has faded, and there are no means on the open downs of knowing whether the direction pursued is right or wrong, till a boulder (which is a landmark) is perceived.
>
> (Richard Jefferies, *The Open Air*, 1885)

The movements of the first people who came to Britain were influenced by climate, the changing seasons and the abundance of food. As they travelled, they would have noticed natural landmarks along their route: a hill with a distinctive profile, a boulder abandoned by a glacier, or a system of caves gouged out by meltwater. As cultures and practices evolved, and the possession of land became a desirable asset, landmarks helped to define territorial boundaries. Like the features of a much-loved face, they gave a sense of belonging.

We also began to interpret the landscape in a different way – one that was richly imaginative. Storytelling is a natural human instinct, and when these stories were woven around topographical features they became fused into our perception of the world around us. These tales helped to answer our darkest questions about life and death. They explained our past, describing gods and heroes who had inhabited this land before; they taught important lessons about qualities such as courage, honour, loyalty, jealousy, revenge and forgiveness; and they brought the spirit world almost within touching distance, so that it seemed ever-present and all-powerful.

Over time, the most ancient man-made relics – standing stones, hill forts or chalk figures – became landmarks too, their origins half-submerged in a multitude of vivid legends that reflected the superstitions of successive generations. Some very old pagan practices have survived to this day, giving us a glimpse into the minds of the first people to settle here. In the 17th century, while the antiquarian John Aubrey was visiting some of these sites and studying their physical remains, he also jotted down the folk tales connected with them. He explained: 'I know that some will nauseate these old Fables: but I doe profess to regard them as the most considerable pieces of Antiquity I collect.' (*Monumenta Britannica*, 1665–93.)

One gift that these legends give us is a personal reconnection with the landscape.

Inevitably, as new cultures and beliefs arrived, some legends were adapted to suit a particular purpose. Christianity introduced saints who battled with the Devil over the location of hilltop churches and imprisoned evil spirits in standing stones. But the wildness of these stories cannot be subdued. From subterranean chambers, vengeful gods with Norse or Saxon names ride out across the sky, their spectral hounds clamouring for lost souls. Dragons lurk in fathomless pools, knights and their horses slumber in secret caves, and colossal ships patrol the seas.

Not all of these stories are ancient. Some were born in comparatively recent times, perhaps inspired by specific people or events, and they raise fascinating questions of their own. What on earth spooked the ferryman one stormy night on Windermere in the 16th century? Why was William Wordsworth tempted to fabricate a legend about a waterfall? Did the Physicians of Myddfai inherit their gifts from a benevolent lake-dwelling nymph, or were they just extremely good at their job?

One gift that these legends give us is a personal reconnection with the landscape, allowing us to be fully present in the here and now, and experience these places just as an unbroken line of humans have experienced them before us. Admittedly, many landmarks have changed over the centuries, and some now receive large numbers of visitors, but it is still possible to feel something of their energy. (Just how strongly we want to do so is worth considering, particularly in places such as Chanctonbury Ring and Ben Macdui.)

Of course, the oldest of these stories were spoken aloud before they were ever written down. Families would have sat spellbound around a fire as the voice of a bard brought them vividly to life. By nature they are fluid and alive, constantly changing and evolving as we ourselves change and evolve, but if we try too hard to analyse them they dance away from our fingers – like King Arthur himself, who has so far confounded our best efforts to bring him into the 'real' world.

Instead, if we hope to glimpse the elusive characters who walked before us across this endlessly varied landscape, we must try and recapture the open-minded curiosity of Dan and Una, who conjured Puck out of Pook's Hill just by the sheer pleasure of retelling an old story, while the shadows of evening fell across a summer meadow.

An important note about access

Many of the landmarks described in this book are open to the public – indeed, a number of them are in the care of the National Trust, and more information can be found on their website. However, a few are located on private land with no public right of access, and it is essential to obtain permission from relevant landowners or authorities before attempting to visit them in person. Where public access is possible, some places still necessitate an arduous trek over difficult terrain – especially those in Wales and Scotland. I would strongly advise you to steer clear of Dunmail Raise, because it stands in the central reservation of a dual carriageway.

I have deliberately included a few landmarks that survive only in legend. I don't believe that this precludes us from seeing them, at least in our imagination. If you are in Cornwall or Ceredigion, and you find yourself gazing out to sea on a calm day, you might still hear the muted pealing of church bells or catch a glimpse of distant spires.

SOUTH WEST ENGLAND

ST MICHAEL'S MOUNT

Writing in his *Bibliotecha historica* in the 1st century AD, the Greek historian Diodorus Siculus described how the people living in a part of Britain called Belerion were expert at mining and smelting tin; at low tide they would take wagonloads of this metal to an island called Ictis, where it was purchased by merchants and shipped away to the Mediterranean.

It is possible that Diodorus Siculus obtained his information from the accounts (now lost) of a Greek navigator and geographer called Pytheas, who sailed around the British Isles in the 4th century BC. 'Belerion' is an old name for the area around Land's End, and, in view of Cornwall's long history of tin-mining, some historians believe that the island of Ictis could be St Michael's Mount, an island in Mount's Bay which is accessible via a causeway during ebb tide.

One of the original objections to this theory was the local tradition that, in the distant past, St Michael's Mount was a landlocked hill that stood in the middle of a forest; its old Cornish name, *Karrek Loos yn Koos* ('the grey rock in the wood'), backs up this story, as does the regular appearance, at very low tide, of the stumps and roots of ancient trees still buried in the sand. But scientific analysis of these trees indicates that the forest was submerged by the sea at least 1,500 years before Pytheas' voyage; it seems that folklore has a very long memory.*

---

* This submerged forest was seen by some writers as supplementary evidence for the existence of Lyonesse (see p. 20), a legendary kingdom that was engulfed by the sea.

Living in this forest, so generations of parents have told their wide-eyed children, was a formidable giant named Cormoran and his wife, Cormelian. Cormoran wanted to build a fortress on the Mount, but he was lazy and ordered his wife to go and fetch some stone for it. He demanded white granite, which occurred a long way away, but Cormelian waited until her husband was asleep and collected some local greenstone instead. As she was tiptoeing past Cormoran, he suddenly woke up and saw her; at that moment her apron strings broke and she dropped the entire load. The result can still be seen, in the form of Chapel Rock, not far from the Mount.

Cormoran made such a nuisance of himself by preying on herds of cattle that the local villagers were in despair. One of them, named Jack, hatched a plan. He dug a deep pit in the sand, disguised it with branches, waited until nightfall and then blew his horn, which he knew would bring out the giant. Cormoran ran straight into the trap and perished. Jack, who was celebrated thereafter as 'Jack the Giant Killer', was rewarded with a sword and a belt embroidered with the words: 'Here's the right valiant Cornish man / Who slew the giant Cormoran.'

According to tradition, the Mount's connection with Saint Michael began in the late 5th century AD, when seafarers reported seeing a glowing apparition of Saint Michael on the west side of the island, warning them away from its dangerous rocks. The island, and the 'chair' in which Saint Michael appeared, soon became a place of pilgrimage, and in the 11th century Edward the Confessor founded a monastery here. This became a daughter-house to the Benedictine monastery on Mont St Michel in

Brittany – an island which in many respects is the 'twin' of St Michael's Mount, even down to its own legend of a submerged kingdom.

> Marked ye the Angel-spectre that appeared?
> By other hands the holy fane is reared
> High on the point, where, gazing o'er the flood,
> Confessed, the glittering apparition stood.
> And now the sailor, on his watch of night,
> Sees, like a glimmering star, the far-off light;
> Or, homeward bound, hears on the twilight bay
> The slowly-chanted vespers die away!

> (William Lisle Bowles, 'St Michael's Mount',
> *The Poetical Works of William Lisle Bowles*, 1855)

There are Arthurian links here, too. At a market on St Michael's Mount, so legend tells us, a benevolent hermit named Ogrin purchased new clothes and a horse for Queen Isolde, who was dressed in rags after fleeing into the wilds with her lover, Tristan (these characters are also connected with Tintagel and Lyonesse – see pp. 16 and 20). King Arthur and his knights are also said to sleep beneath the Mount, and will only wake and ride out to battle when Albion's plight is desperate.

Today, thousands of visitors and pilgrims still cross the cobbled tidal causeway to the island and make the breathless climb to explore the church and the fortified castle which, for centuries, has been the home of the St Aubyn family. It was from the church tower that the first beacon was lit to warn of the approach of the Spanish Armada in 1588, and, during the Napoleonic Wars in the early 1800s, cannon fire from the castle walls blew the masts off a French ship that ventured too close to the English coast.

TINTAGEL

On a wave-lashed island, which is hanging on to the mainland of north Cornwall by a mere thread of crumbling rock, stand the remains of a once-great castle. Here, according to legend, King Arthur was conceived; and some stories say that he died here too, surrounded by his knights, after being shot by a poisoned arrow at the Battle of Camlann.

It is to the chronicler Geoffrey of Monmouth that we owe the earliest written connection of Tintagel with King Arthur. Writing in his *Historia regum Britanniae* (c. 1136), he tells us that Arthur's father was a king named Uther Pendragon, who was in love with a beautiful and virtuous woman called Igraine. Igraine was married to Gorlois, the Duke of Cornwall, but such was Uther's passion that his desire was obvious to everyone in his court. Enraged at the king's behaviour, Gorlois placed Igraine in the safety of his fortress at Tintagel.

Uther besieged Tintagel, but to no avail. In desperation he persuaded the sorcerer, Merlin, to transform him into an exact likeness of Gorlois so that he could make love to Igraine while her husband was away. This is how Arthur was conceived, and as King of the Britons he grew up to fight a series of fierce battles against the invading Anglo-Saxons, resulting in temporary victory but culminating in tragic defeat.

The problem faced by historians is that Geoffrey of Monmouth was writing some 700 years after Arthur is said to have existed, and he liked to embellish fact with fiction. At Tintagel, no trace of Gorlois' castle has ever been found. And yet ... in recent years, excavation of what was thought to be a modest 5th-century settlement has yielded pieces of high-status glass and pottery, including Roman amphorae, hinting at a much more significant and prestigious community with links to the Mediterranean. Cornwall, in the Roman era, was a valuable source of tin, and with its sheltered harbour Tintagel was ideally situated for ships engaged in a profitable trade.

In view of this fresh evidence, it has been suggested that Tintagel was a royal site in the 5th and 6th centuries – perhaps a stronghold of the rulers of Dumnonia, a kingdom in South West England. It is possible that Geoffrey of Monmouth had heard folklore about Tintagel as a place of strategic importance and combined it with stories of King Arthur, which were current in Cornwall by the early 12th century.

Following in Geoffrey's wake came new generations of storytellers and another legend grew up about Tintagel. In this legend, it is the seat of King Mark of Cornwall. When Mark's nephew, Tristan*, is asked to escort Isolde, an Irish princess, to Tintagel so that she can marry the king, Tristan falls in love with her himself and the couple engage in an affair right under the king's nose. When they are discovered, the king imprisons Tristan in a cliff-top chapel, but he escapes and races to find Isolde; they gallop to safety in a forest and shelter in a cave, but their hopes of happiness are soon torn apart by tragedy.

In 1233, this romantic story beguiled the new owner of Tintagel into building a castle that was a real-life theatrical setting for Tristan and Isolde. Richard, Earl of Cornwall, was the wealthy

* See Lyonesse (p. 20) for the full story of Tristan and Isolde.

younger brother of King Henry III, and his opulent design included a walled garden, where the lovers were supposed to have met in secret, and a chapel from which Tristan leapt to freedom. The ruins of Richard's castle are the most substantial structural remains that survive on the island of Tintagel today.

So, in Tintagel we have a 5th-century settlement that may have inspired a legend, which inspired a 13th-century castle that perpetuated the legend. How can historical fact be teased out from such a tangle?

In the 19th century, Alfred, Lord Tennyson gave it the full Gothic treatment and imagined fresh scenarios. In his *Idylls of the King* (1859), King Leodogran of Cameliard enlists Arthur's help in battle and afterwards Arthur seeks permission to marry the king's daughter, Guinevere. Suspicious about Arthur's ancestry, Leodogran questions Bellicent, Queen of Orkney and half-sister to Arthur. Bellicent recounts a curious tale that she was told by a sorcerer who was an attendant of Uther. On the night that Uther died in Tintagel Castle, still yearning for the heir he thought he lacked, the sorcerer went down to the shore with his protégé, Merlin, and saw a strange, bright ship in the shape of a dragon. As they stood and gazed out to sea, a weird thing happened:

> *Arthur 'almost certainly' existed, and his headquarters had been found.*

Wave after wave, each mightier than the last,
Till last, a ninth one, gathering half the deep
And full of voices, slowly rose and plunged
Roaring, and all the wave was in a flame:
And down the wave and in the flame was borne
A naked babe, and rode to Merlin's feet,
Who stoopt and caught the babe, and cried
'The King! Here is an heir for Uther!'

But where is Arthur now? In 1998, it appeared that his name was written in large letters on a stone with a Latin inscription that was uncovered at Tintagel. Dating from the 6th century, the stone bore the name 'Artognou'. In full, it said: 'Artognou, father of a descendant of Coll, had this constructed.' The media went wild: Arthur 'almost certainly' existed, and his headquarters had been found. The trouble was that 'Artognou' is not the same as Arthur, which, in Latin, would be *Artorius*.

Once again, Arthur eludes us. As always, he is just out of reach – visible only in our mind's eye, lingering in folklore but never solidifying into reality. It's as if we're only allowed to get so close … because, after all, if we proved his existence, how could the legend live?

LYONESSE

The Isles of Scilly lie some 28 miles (45km) south-west of Land's End in Cornwall. The five largest islands are inhabited, while the others comprise around 140 rocky islets, low-lying and wave-battered. At very low tides it is possible to walk between some of the islands. But several thousand years ago, when sea levels were lower, it is believed that they were part of one large land mass whose Cornish name was Lethowsow. This became known in folklore as Lyonesse.

In a tradition that echoes that of Cantre'r Gwaelod (see p. 159) in Cardigan Bay (Bae Ceredigion), Lyonesse was said to be a rich and fertile country, with no fewer than 140 churches and a fair city called Lyons. But one night a storm sent an enormous wave crashing over its shores, permanently inundating the land and drowning its inhabitants. Afterwards, around a submerged reef called the Seven Stones, fishermen would occasionally haul up fragments of ruined buildings in their nets, and in rough weather the muffled pealing of church bells could be heard beneath the waves.

One man is said to have survived the deluge by leaping onto his white horse and galloping ahead of the wave. This survivor is claimed as an ancestor by two Cornish families: in the 1811 edition of Richard Carew's *Survey of Cornwall* (1602), editor Thomas Tonkin reveals in a footnote that both the Trevilian (Trevelyan) and the Vyvyan families bear on their crest a horse emerging from the waves. He adds that the name Vyvyan, in the old Cornish tongue, means 'to flee away'.

In Thomas Malory's 15th-century collection of Arthurian tales called *Le Morte d'Arthur*, Lyonesse is the birthplace of Sir Tristan, one of King Arthur's knights. Tristan's father, Meliodas, is described as 'lord and king of the country of Liones'. (*Le Morte d'Arthur*, ed. Sir Edward Strachey, 1919.) Tristan is sent away from Lyonesse while he is still a boy and he grows up to play a leading role in one of the most iconic love stories of all time.

Tristan is tasked with escorting an Irish princess called Isolde (or Iseult) to Cornwall, where she is destined to marry Tristan's uncle, the Cornish king. Isolde carries with her a love potion to ensure a happy marriage with her future husband, but during the voyage she and Tristan drink it by accident, and they fall hopelessly in love.

From the beginning, the lovers are doomed. After Isolde's wedding to King Mark of Cornwall, she and Tristan continue to meet in secret until they are discovered. Narrowly escaping a death sentence, Isolde returns to Ireland, while Tristan is exiled to Brittany. There he meets and marries another princess called Isolde ('Isolde of the White Hands'). The marriage is unhappy and when Tristan is wounded in battle he sends for his first love, who has the power of healing.

Tristan has requested that, as the ship arrives in Brittany, it should raise white sails if Isolde is aboard and black sails if she is

> *Tristan is sent away from Lyonesse while he is still a boy and he grows up to play a leading role in one of the most iconic love stories of all time.*

not. As he lies on his sickbed, he asks his wife to watch for its approach. She is jealous of her rival and when she sees a ship with white sails she tells her husband that they are black. Believing that his beloved Isolde cares nothing for him, Tristan dies. When she discovers his body, she dies of a broken heart.

Whether or not the Scilly Isles are the remnants of Lyonesse, they have abundant evidence of prehistoric settlement.

Bearing in mind that Cornwall's sunken land was known as Lethowsow, how was it identified as Malory's 'country of Liones'? The antiquary Richard Carew was among the first to make the connection. Citing eyewitness accounts of submerged buildings, he wrote: '... the encroaching sea hath ravined [Cornwall] from the whole country of Lioness ... and that such a Lioness there was, these proofs are yet remaining. The space between the Land's End and the Isles of Scilly, being about thirty miles, to this day retaineth that name, in Cornish *Lethowsow* ....' (*Survey of Cornwall*, 1602.)

Although Lyonesse is now firmly rooted in Cornish folklore, some historians have since suggested that Malory's 'Liones' was the Old French *Loenois,* meaning Lothian in Scotland, while others claim that it was Leonois in Brittany. Confusingly, Brittany has its own legend of a sunken city, and storytellers may have carried this tale to Cornwall where it found a new identity.

Whether or not the Scilly Isles are the remnants of Lyonesse, they have abundant evidence of prehistoric settlement. Early Bronze Age inhabitants left a rich legacy of cairns, standing stones and entrance graves, but their available land was already being eaten away by rising sea levels. This process seems to have been gradual, rather than sudden and catastrophic. In the Roman era the Isles of Scilly were probably still one large island, but within a few centuries the central plain had been flooded and several smaller islands had been formed.

Generations of writers have been captivated by the legend of a lost land, its Arthurian connection, and the sense of some distant, overwhelming tragedy. In his epic poem *Idylls of the King* (1859), Alfred, Lord Tennyson chose Lyonesse as the setting for King Arthur's heroic death in what he called 'this last, dim, weird battle of the west':

> Then rose the King and moved his host by night,
> And ever push'd Sir Modred, league by league,
> Back to the sunset bound of Lyonnesse –
> A land of old upheaven from the abyss
> By fire, to sink into the abyss again;
> Where fragments of forgotten peoples dwelt,
> And the long mountains ended in a coast
> Of ever-shifting sand, and far away
> The phantom circle of a moaning sea.

BRENTOR

Devonshire folklore speaks of a time long ago when an English merchant was returning to his native shores. He had left his homeland as a young man and made his fortune in spices and silks. He was looking forward to spending his remaining years amid the green and rolling landscape he knew as a boy, but, as his ship approached Devon's south coast, a violent storm blew up, sending waves crashing over the deck and threatening to drive it against the cliffs.

In desperation, the merchant prayed to Saint Michael, patron saint of mariners, and vowed that if the ship was spared he would build a church on the first land he saw. The storm subsided and when the sky cleared his gaze alighted on the cone-shaped hill of Brent Tor (or Brentor). True to his word, he gathered the necessary stones, carried them up to the summit and built a chapel dedicated to Saint Michael, which still stands as a testament to his gratitude.

This is just one explanation for the origin of the tiny church of St Michael de Rupe (St Michael of the Rock), which sits atop a 1,100-foot (335-metre) hill on the western edge of Dartmoor National Park. Another story, recounted by Anna Eliza Bray in *Traditions, Legends, Superstitions and Sketches of Devonshire* (1838), claims that the villagers began to build the church at the foot of the hill, but the Devil repeatedly moved the stones overnight to the summit. Seeing their trouble, Saint Michael hurled a massive rock at the Devil, who stayed well clear, and meanwhile the church was completed on the hilltop.

The most historically accurate version is that the church was founded in 1130 by Robert Giffard, a local landowner. Measuring just 37 feet (11 metres) in length and seating around 40 people, it is considered to be the highest working church in southern England. Although it stands well inland, its visibility from the sea is mentioned in Sabine Baring-Gould's Gothic horror story, *Margery of Quether* (1891): 'We loved the little old church; it was seen by Drake and Raleigh as they sailed into Plymouth Sound ....'

In Baring-Gould's tale, the narrator, George Rosedhu, climbs Brentor at midnight on Christmas Eve to ring the church bells. In the darkness a tiny, wizened woman with bat-like claws descends from the bell-rope and latches onto him; George describes how she proceeds to 'extract ... the blood from my veins and the marrow from my bones, and assimilate it herself'.

> *Its many names, including Burnt Tor and Beacon Tor, suggest that signal fires were lit here in ancient times.*

In more recent times it has been suggested that Baring-Gould's stories helped to inspire Bram Stoker's *Dracula,* first published in 1897.

Unlike most of Devon's tors, which are formed of granite, Brentor is a mound of basalt, created when volcanic lava flowed into the sea some 350 million years ago. Its summit is encircled by the earthworks of an Iron Age hill fort, and its many names, including Burnt Tor and Beacon Tor, suggest that signal fires were lit here in ancient times, perhaps warning of imminent invasion.

On a clear day, Brentor offers wide-reaching views across

Dartmoor, Bodmin Moor and the Tamar Valley. But setting aside the romantic folk tales, it's hard to disagree with the writer Henry Edmund Carrington, who wrote: 'We find it difficult to account for the erection of a place of worship on so wild and exposed a site.' (*The Plymouth and Devonport Guide*, 1828.)

It was the 17th-century antiquary John Aubrey who observed that most churches dedicated to Saint Michael either stood on high ground, or else had a tall tower or steeple. He wondered whether this was because, according to the New Testament, Saint Michael and his angels defeated Lucifer and cast him out of heaven, meaning that Saint Michael was regarded as the natural saint to oppose the Devil in high places. In recent years this curious phenomenon has been noticed afresh by Earth-energy diviners, who have plotted a 'Michael line' stretching right across southern and eastern Britain; this incorporates a surprising number of hilltop churches dedicated to Saint Michael, including St Michael's Mount, Glastonbury and Brentor.

In his book *The View Over Atlantis* (1969), John Michell discusses whether, in ages past, this line was believed to be the pathway of an unseen 'dragon current' of energy; he wonders whether Saint Michael has supplanted an earlier 'guardian' of that current, and suggests that the traditional representations of Saint Michael killing a dragon are symbolic of his control over an elemental force.

Perhaps, as the poet N.T. Carrington suggests, Brentor remembers a wilder time, long before our own:

And here, as sages say, in days long flown,—
Here, on this stormy, barren, blasted ridge,
Luxuriant forests rose; and far away
Swept the bold hills beneath the gazer's eye
In beautiful succession, dark with leaf,—
An ocean of refreshing verdure toss'd
By gales Atlantic. In the upland grove,
With independence bless'd, and sylvan ease,
Our fathers lov'd to dwell; and here they form'd
The rude encampment, and the rural home,
While the gaunt wolf and winged serpent held
Dominion o'er the vales.

('Dartmoor', *The Collected Poems of N.T. Carrington*,
Vol. I, 1834)

WISTMAN'S WOOD

Few places in Britain are more wild and desolate than Dartmoor,
with its high, exposed granite tors, its rain-soaked moorlands and
treacherous expanses of bog. Because of the severity of the winds
that scour the landscape, any trees that grow here must be hardy
and well-adapted to their environment, and nowhere is this better
seen than in the damp, mossy, bewitching underworld of
Wistman's Wood.

· This precious 9-acre (3.5-hectare) woodland sits at an altitude
of 1,300 feet (400 metres) and is one of the few remnants of
upland oakwood that have survived on Dartmoor since
prehistoric times. Most of the individual trees have been growing

here for no more than about 200 years, but they appear much older, their gnarled forms bent low to the ground like lurking beasts, waiting to trip unwary feet with their green-carpeted grasping arms.

Flourishing in this lush environment are all kinds of lichens, ferns and mosses, and the delicate powder-blue trumpets of ivy-leaved bellflower push upwards between the boulders. In spring, redstarts and spotted flycatchers build their cup-shaped nests in the branches.

But at night, according to folklore, something rather more sinister stirs in the heart of Wistman's Wood: a pack of bloodthirsty spectral dogs called the Wisht Hounds, who run baying across the moors in search of unbaptised human souls.

This terrifying spectacle was also known in the West Country as the Yeth Hounds or the Yell Hounds, and on stormy nights they could be heard in full cry, along with the blast of a hunter's horn. The huntsman or leader of the hounds was sometimes identified as a character called Old Crockern – in Sabine Baring-Gould's *A Book of the West* (1900), a Dartmoor resident warns a newcomer to beware of 'the gurt old sperit of the moors, old Crockern himself, grey as granite, and his eyebrows hanging down over his glimmering eyes like sedge, and his eyes deep as peat water pools'.

Folklorists connect the story of the Wisht Hounds with the Wild Hunt, a long-standing tradition that is found in many places throughout Britain and Northern Europe. This phantom cavalcade of horsemen and hounds was believed to ride across the night sky, snatching up lost souls. In Norse mythology the Wild Hunt was led by Odin – the god of war, known to the Anglo-Saxons as Woden – and to hear or see it was a portent of ill fortune or death.

As an example of the malevolence of the Wisht Hounds, an old tale described how, late one night, a farmer was riding back from Widecombe Fair. He heard a pack of hounds approaching and turned to see the dark shape of a huntsman at their head. Believing him to be a local rider, and half-hoping to be offered a share of the bag, he called out to ask how the hunt had gone. For answer, the rider tossed him a large bundle and the farmer hurried home gratefully. But when he unwrapped it, he was horrified to find the body of his infant son.

It has been suggested that the words 'Wisht' and 'Wistman' may both originate from 'whisht', which in local dialect means 'eerie' or 'haunted'. In her book *Traditions, Legends, Superstitions and Sketches of Devonshire* (1838), Anna Eliza Bray claimed that Wistman's Wood meant 'a wood of wisemen', and referred to an old belief that it was a meeting-place of druids. Just to enhance the air of mystery, an ancient coffin road known as the Lych Way passes near its northern edge; centuries ago, corpses were carried along this route for burial at Lydford Church, and in more recent years witnesses have reported seeing a procession of monks in white habits treading the path in ghostly silence.

The crime writer Sir Arthur Conan Doyle drew on the legend of the Wisht Hounds when he penned his classic mystery *The Hound of the Baskervilles* (1902). When Sherlock Holmes' trusty assistant, Dr Watson, ventures out onto Dartmoor at night in the company of local landowner Sir Henry Baskerville, he hears a noise that makes his blood run cold: 'It came with the wind through the silence of the night, a long, deep mutter, then a rising howl, and then the sad moan in which it died away. Again and again it sounded, the whole air throbbing with it, strident, wild, and menacing.'

CORFE CASTLE

On 18 March 978, the young King Edward was on horseback,
galloping over Dorset's Purbeck Hills. Dusk was falling; he had
enjoyed a day's hunting and had become separated from the other
riders as they returned from the chase. It occurred to him that his
younger half-brother, Aethelred, was staying nearby in the royal
residence at Corfe. On impulse, he decided to call and see him
before he rejoined the huntsmen. It was a decision that cost him
his life.

As Edward approached the gate of the Saxon hall, Aethelred's
mother, Elfrida, came out to greet him. She invited him to
dismount but he refused,
explaining that he had merely
dropped by to see his brother.
Elfrida insisted that he take
some refreshment and a cup of
wine was quickly brought out.
Aethelred had still not
appeared; Edward reached

*In the 11th century, one
of the first stone-built
Norman castles was
raised here by William
the Conqueror.*

down for the cup and, as he did so, one of Elfrida's attendants
grabbed his hand and pulled it forwards as if to give him a kiss of
welcome. Then another man seized his left arm and stabbed him
in the back.

Edward was only 15 or 16. He had been crowned two years
previously, after the sudden and unexpected death of his father,
Edgar the Peaceful. But his accession was not universally accepted
and one of his strongest opponents was Elfrida, Edgar's widow.

Elfrida is believed to have been Edgar's third wife; the quick disposal of his second wife into a nunnery, to make way for the beautiful and ambitious Elfrida, had led Dunstan, Archbishop of Canterbury, to accuse Edgar of adultery. Edward was the offspring of Edgar's first marriage but Elfrida was determined to secure the crown for her own son.

Some accounts claim that Elfrida herself delivered the fatal blow. Whether or not this is true, the unfortunate Edward was dragged for some distance with his foot caught in his horse's stirrup. From then onwards, the story is blurred with superstition and folklore. That night, a servant was sent from the castle to find the king's body and conceal it. He took it first to the house of a blind woman, but around midnight she found her sight miraculously restored and her house filled with brilliant light. Hearing of this, Elfrida then ordered that Edward's body be thrown into a well; meanwhile she hastily removed herself from the scene of the crime. The body was later discovered, with a pillar of light illuminating its resting place. Thereafter, the king became known as Edward the Martyr and many miracles of healing were ascribed to the well's water.

Edward's body was buried quietly in Wareham, but within a year it was disinterred and found to be in a state of miraculous preservation – a recognised sign of saintliness. He was reburied in Shaftesbury Abbey but, according to legend, his scheming stepmother Elfrida found it physically impossible to attend the ceremony: every horse she mounted would only walk backwards. Maybe she was stricken with remorse, but she had achieved her objective of placing her son, Aethelred, on the throne. His reign was neither happy nor glorious: as Aethelred the Unready (from the Old English *Unraed*, or 'ill-advised') he was unable to repel the ambitions of the Danes, who already occupied a swathe of eastern England and had their eyes on the crown.

This blood-soaked drama happened before the present castle at Corfe was even built. The *Anglo-Saxon Chronicle* records Edward's murder at a place called Corfe, and his story was later embellished by medieval historians, including William of Malmesbury and Henry of Huntingdon. In the 11th century, one of the first stone-built Norman castles was raised here by William the Conqueror and the structure survived for hundreds of years.

When the Civil War broke out in the 17th century, Corfe Castle was owned by Sir John Bankes, Attorney General to King Charles I. In May 1643, while Sir John was away in the service of the King, his wife, Lady Mary, successfully held Corfe Castle with a small garrison against a siege by Parliamentarians. However, during a second siege in 1645, a member of the garrison secretly allowed the enemy forces in. Lady Mary was allowed the keys to the castle, but the castle itself had its walls undermined, packed with gunpowder and blown up. The large metal keys are displayed in the library of the new Bankes family home, Kingston Lacy.

The shattered towers of Corfe Castle still have a commanding presence, rising like broken teeth from the steep mound which has always offered such a superb natural defence. In the Iron Age there may have been a hill fort here, and finds of pottery show that Castle Hill was occupied in the Roman period when the diverse geology of Purbeck was quarried for clay, limestone, shale and salt. A phantom army is said to trace the footsteps of Roman soldiers: in December 1678, a group of local people were horrified to witness thousands of soldiers advancing across the Purbeck Hills amid much clashing of weapons. They ran to rouse the people of Wareham, where the militia was called out, and a local squire galloped to warn the Privy Council in London of imminent invasion. However, nothing more was seen of the mysterious army.

In Thomas Hardy's novel *The Hand of Ethelberta* (1876), Corfe Castle appears as Coomb Castle (Corvsgate in later editions). Ethelberta, who is an aspiring poet, rides on a donkey to attend a meeting amid the castle ruins but is distracted by their romantic decay: 'Once among the towers above, she became so interested in the windy corridors, mildewed dungeons, and the tribe of daws [jackdaws] peering invidiously upon her from overhead, that she forgot the flight of time.'

Alongside Hardy's 'tribe of daws', ravens have long been a familiar sight among the ruins of Corfe Castle. A superstition warns that, if they should leave, disaster will follow, and this seems to have been borne out by their disappearance before the Civil War. They made a welcome return, however, and the Dorset naturalist Reginald Bosworth Smith recalled how, in the mid-1800s, ravens nested in 'perhaps the most fitting place of all – on the ruins of Corfe Castle.' (*Bird Life and Bird Lore*, 1905.) Bosworth Smith lamented the disastrous effects of persecution, adding: 'What would not Corfe Castle ... gain in impressiveness, if there were ravens there still?' Thankfully, in more recent years, ravens have nested regularly in the castle's keep.

CERNE GIANT

Looming large on a hillside above the village of Cerne Abbas in Dorset is a chalk figure known as the Cerne Giant. He stands 200 feet (60 metres) tall, is stark naked and wields a club rather menacingly in his right hand. However, his most eye-catching feature – a 36-foot (11-metre) erect penis – is what has gained him the most attention over the centuries, from archaeologists puzzling over his original purpose to casual visitors eager to be scandalised (or awestruck, depending upon their inclination).

Historians have wondered whether the Cerne Giant was an Iron Age pagan fertility god or perhaps a Roman-era figure of Hercules – or even an amalgam of the two, as an earlier figure could have been tailored to suit the preference of Britons under Roman rule. The Roman theory was particularly convincing, as the Giant holds

Fresh scientific analysis placed the Cerne Giant in a different era altogether.

his left arm as if something was once draped over it – and Hercules traditionally carries the skin of the Nemean lion, which he killed as his first 'labour', over his left arm.

Another school of thought claimed that the Giant was relatively recent and had been etched into the landscape on the orders of Lord Holles of Dorchester Priory, an influential statesman during the Civil War who initially fought with the Parliamentarians but then argued for a peaceful settlement with

King Charles I. This idea also made sense, because Cromwell was known derisively as 'the English Hercules'.

But in 2021, these theories had to be abandoned when fresh scientific analysis placed the Cerne Giant in a different era altogether. Using a technique called optically stimulated luminescence dating, which examined samples from the deepest layers of chalk to see when they were last exposed to sunlight, the figure was placed within a timeframe of between AD 700 and 1100. There is no written evidence of the Giant before the late 1600s, so the current thinking is that he may have been neglected for several centuries before being rediscovered and recut.

This new evidence means that the Giant could have been created around the same time as Cerne Abbey, a Benedictine monastery which was founded in AD 987. There is a story that the abbey was set up to discourage the local people from worshipping an Anglo-Saxon god called Helith, which suggests that the Giant may be a depiction of him. But, somewhat mysteriously, there is no mention of the Giant in surviving documents from Cerne Abbey.

Folklore tells of how the Christian missionary Saint Augustine arrived in the district intent on evangelising, but residents refused to abandon their pagan beliefs; they tied fish tails (or cows' tails) to his clothing and drove him away, amid torrents of ribald abuse. In retaliation, Saint Augustine prayed that all the children born to the culprits would have tails, and, when this happened, they begged his forgiveness and asked him to come back and baptise them. Saint Augustine struck his staff into the ground and a spring of healing water miraculously gushed forth; he named the place Cernel, from the Latin *cerno* ('I perceive') and the Hebrew *El*, one of the Old Testament names for God.

On the hilltop above the Giant there is a banked earthwork believed to date from the Iron Age. This is called the Trendle, and it is a traditional venue for May Day dancing and revelry. According to snippets of folklore collected in 1897, a maypole freshly cut from a fir tree was brought here every year and was always set up at night in readiness for May morning. The Trendle is still the site of May Day festivities, although a maypole is no longer erected.

A long-standing local belief claims that the Giant will bestow fertility; people who wish to have children walk around his outline, or even sleep there overnight. Another old story describes how the figure was once a flesh and blood giant who rampaged around the neighbourhood and feasted on herds of cattle. The villagers waited until he lay down on the hillside to sleep and then tethered him to the ground, like Gulliver in *Gulliver's Travels*, before killing him. They chalked around his corpse so that they would never forget their triumph. All things considered, it seems that the people of Cerne Abbas were a force to be reckoned with.

Thomas Hardy might well have been aware of this tale when he wrote his drama *The Dynasts* (1910), which is set partly in Wessex during the Napoleonic Wars. Exchanging banter with two local men who are keeping a look-out for invaders, Dorset woman Keziar Cantle shares some gruesome gossip about

There is evidence to suggest that in the late 1700s he had a navel.

Napoleon: 'They say that he lives upon human flesh, and has rashers o' baby every morning for breakfast – for all the world like the Cernel Giant in old ancient times!'

There are puzzles yet to be solved about the Giant: for instance, whether the figure has changed shape or moved slightly over time. There is evidence to suggest that in the late 1700s he had a navel, but since then his penis seems to have been lengthened to incorporate it. He is now in the care of the National Trust and the 'scouring' of the figure, which involves the hammering-in of between 15 and 17 tonnes of fresh chalk, is undertaken at regular intervals to prevent it from becoming overgrown.

BADBURY RINGS

Dorset is peppered with over 30 Iron Age hill forts and Badbury Rings is considered to be one of the finest. Rising to a height of 327 feet (100 metres) above sea level, it consists of three concentric ramparts and ditches, and offers fabulous views over the surrounding countryside. In summer the grass is studded with orchids, and butterflies dance in the sunshine while skylarks pour out their songs overhead.

Badbury has long been associated with the legend of King Arthur, largely because its name is thought to preserve an echo of Arthur's twelfth and greatest battle against the Anglo-Saxons. According to Nennius' *History of the Britons* (c. 830), this was the battle of Mons Badonicus or Badon Hill, during which, Nennius claims, Arthur single-handedly felled 960 of his foes in a single day. Another source, *The Annals of Wales* (a 12th-century copy of a presumed 10th-century manuscript), states that during the battle Arthur carried the cross of Christ on his shoulders for three days and nights, and that his army of Britons was victorious.

Although the written details are sparse, some historians looking to place the battlefield on the map have been drawn to Badbury by the folklore that connects it with Badon Hill. In his *Origines Celticae* (1883), Edwin Guest wrote: 'Why may not the Mons Badonicus be the Badbury of Dorsetshire? Its elevated site, its great strength and evident importance, and its name, all alike favour the hypothesis.'

The oldest artefacts discovered here are flint tools dating from the early Neolithic period of 6,000 years ago, and close by are a number of Bronze Age barrows. Construction of the hill fort began around 500 or 600 BC. From about 100 BC, its occupants are thought to have been the Durotriges – a Celtic tribe who lived in parts of South West England.

Visual reconstructions of Iron Age settlements evoke an atmosphere of rural harmony, with smoke curling lazily from wide conical thatches. In reality, life may have been less than idyllic. After AD 43, any peace was permanently shattered by the sight of Roman soldiers advancing on hill forts throughout South West England. We can only imagine with what horror the Durotriges stood and watched the approach of the Second Augustan Legion, commanded by the future emperor Vespasian. There is no knowing how much resistance they offered, but it is clear that Badbury was abandoned around this time.

> *There have been claims that the ghosts of Arthur and his knights ride around Badbury Rings.*

Assuming that King Arthur might have flourished in the late 5th or early 6th century, is there any physical evidence to suggest his presence at Badbury Rings? Excavations by National Trust archaeologists have yielded evidence of reoccupation between AD 480 and 540, offering a tantalising but all-too-flimsy hope that it heard the clash of Arthurian swords.

The early 20th-century writer Mary Butts, a native of Dorset, was a frequent visitor to Badbury Rings and it inspired the name of her 1925 novel, *Ashe of Rings*. Lying on the grass of the hill fort, Butts believed she could detect its latent magic. She wrote: 'It is said of this place that in the time of Arthur, the legendary king of Britain, Morgan le Fay, an enchantress of the period, had dealings of an inconceivable nature there. Today the country people will not approach it at night, not even the hardiest shepherd.'

There have been claims that the ghosts of Arthur and his knights ride around Badbury Rings, perhaps re-enacting their glorious victory at Badon Hill. Some observers have been struck by the sight of ravens there, because the birds are said to embody the spirit of King Arthur. Edwin Guest was convinced of their significance and wrote: '... in view of the ancient superstition that the dead hero's soul passed into a raven ... it is curious to read that the solitary clump of trees which now crowns the hill was the haunt of the last pair of ravens to linger in Wessex.' (*Origines Celticae,* 1883.)

Guest was unduly pessimistic, because today ravens are a regular sight around Badbury – proving nothing, of course, but reminding us nonetheless of 'the once and future king'.

GLASTONBURY

A place of Christian worship so old that it's rumoured it was visited by Christ himself; a heart-centre of Earth energy inviting spiritual pilgrimage; the resting place of a 'once and future king'; a symbol of England's past and a promise of its future. Glastonbury in Somerset is all these things at once and binds them with a magic so strong that we step eagerly into its web.

The beginning of the Glastonbury legends may lie in a 10th-century text called the *Life of Saint Dunstan*. It describes Glastonbury as a royal island in the kingdom of Athelstan, on which stood an ancient church that was built by no human skill (in other words, by God himself) and was the source of many miracles. Saint Dunstan was an Abbot of Glastonbury and he may have helped to shape this early legend. When he expanded the church he preserved the earlier wooden structure and by the time of his death a belief was springing up that it had been built by Christ's own followers who came to Glastonbury in the 1st century AD.

Soon, this extraordinary claim began to sprout new branches. Chief among these was the story that Joseph of Arimathea, the man who took Christ's body down from the Cross, came to Glastonbury and buried the Holy Grail (the chalice used at the Last Supper) at the foot of Glastonbury Tor. Then, after climbing a nearby hill with his companions, Joseph struck his staff into the ground and exclaimed 'We are weary all!', giving rise both to the name of the place – Wearyall Hill – and to the Glastonbury thorn (a hawthorn tree), which took root from his staff.

Some stories described Joseph as a tin merchant who sailed to Britain on a trading voyage, bringing the young Jesus with him when he visited Glastonbury. This is the tale that inspired William Blake's famous poem, set to music as the hymn 'Jerusalem':

> And did those feet in ancient time
> Walk upon England's mountains green?
> And was the Holy Lamb of God
> On England's pleasant pastures seen?

> (*Milton: A Poem in Two Books*, c. 1808)

The story has a timeless appeal – we want it to be true and we look for evidence to prove it might have happened. It is intriguing to consider that, in the Iron Age, punts were required to navigate Somerset's marshy swamps and Glastonbury may have been accessible by a galley sailing up the River Brue from the Bristol Channel.

There is another legend connected with Glastonbury, and it lies at the heart of England's identity. It seems to have begun, however, as an ingenious publicity exercise. In 1184, fire destroyed the old church; a few years later, the monks dug down into the ground and 'discovered' the skeletons of a man and a woman in a hollowed-out oak tree. With them was a lead cross, bearing a Latin inscription: 'Here lies buried the renowned King Arthur, with Guinevere his second wife, in the Isle of Avalon ....'

By this time, largely thanks to the chronicler Geoffrey of Monmouth, the story of King Arthur was embedded in folklore.

Now, his body had apparently been found; the monks claimed that they had been told to dig there by King Henry II, who himself had been tipped off by a bard in possession of ancient knowledge. The Welsh people, who had been resisting Henry's oppression, happened to believe that the King of Britons was merely sleeping and ready to ride forth in their hour of need. For them in particular, it was bad news to be told that Arthur was actually dead. At the same time, the revelation that Glastonbury was Geoffrey of Monmouth's mystical 'Avalon' seemed like an answer to the monks' most fervent prayers: the bodies were reinterred in an elaborate new tomb, attracting wealthy visitors whose support helped to restore the monastery.

In the centuries that followed, the romances of King Arthur and his knights poured from the pens of gifted writers and an entire pseudo-history was formed, telling of heroic battles, chivalric deeds and an epic quest for the Holy Grail, all painted in the vivid colours of love and betrayal, honour and death ... except that we still preferred to hear that King Arthur did not die: 'Yet some men yet say in many parts of England that king Arthur is not dead, but had by the will of our Lord Jesu into another place. And men say that he shall come again, and he shall win the Holy Cross. I will not say it shall be so ... but many men say that there is written on his tomb this verse: *Hic iacet Arthurus Rex quondam Rex que futurus*.' ('Here lies King Arthur,

> *Whatever we choose to perceive, it is difficult to gaze at the Tor without the stirring of some long-dormant emotion.*

once and future king.') (Thomas Malory, *Le Morte d'Arthur,* 15th century, ed. Sir Edward Strachey, 1868.)

Modern historians have dismissed the discovery of Arthur's body as a clever ploy, but there is no longer any physical evidence to examine. When Glastonbury Abbey was ransacked and destroyed during Henry VIII's Dissolution of the Monasteries, the bones in the tomb were lost. King Arthur's mortal remains – if they ever existed – were whisked safely back into the realm of legend.

The Tor, with its curiously sculpted slopes and its roofless 13th-century tower, has its own secrets. Deep within the hill, so it is said, dwells Gwyn ap Nudd, Lord of Annwn (the Otherworld), guarding the Cauldron of Rebirth. A hidden cave leads to his realm and into this chamber walked the intrepid Saint Collen, a 6th-century wandering saint. He found Gwyn ap Nudd seated in a golden chair and he was offered refreshment – which he refused, because no good ever came of eating fairies' food. Instead, Collen sprinkled holy water around him; in an instant he found himself alone, and in broad daylight, on the bare hillside.

Pilgrims continue to be drawn to Glastonbury by its spiritual landscape. It is said to lie on the Earth's heart chakra, a point where two important lines of Earth energy – the Michael and Mary lines – intersect, and the result can be felt as a gentle but powerful environment of harmony and peace. Whatever we choose to perceive, it is difficult to gaze at the Tor, rising above a sea of mist in the Somerset levels, without the stirring of some long-dormant emotion – the lingering embers, perhaps, of a belief for which we no longer have the words.

CHEDDAR GORGE

England's largest gorge began forming about one million years ago, when a fast-flowing glacial river sliced its way through layers of Carboniferous limestone. Steep cliffs rose on either side of an ever-deepening gorge; when sea levels fell, the Earth's water table dropped too, and the river disappeared underground where it carved out a series of spectacular caves.

Cheddar Gorge is a geological showcase on a dazzling scale, both above and below ground. The Earth's natural processes are still in full flow, as dripping water continues to deposit minerals onto the tips of impressive stalactites and stalagmites, and floodwaters provide a perfect mirror for these creations.

Outside, where rapids once roared through a sinuous canyon, the crags are populated with wild flowers, such as the diminutive Cheddar pink (*Dianthus gratianopolitanus*) which was first discovered here 300 years ago. On the lower slopes, hazel trees provide habitat for dormice, while flourishing high on the cliffs are several unique micro-species of whitebeam trees – including the aptly named *Sorbus cheddarensis*.

Folklore tells a different story about how the gorge was formed. It is said that as the Devil was wandering over the Mendips he decided to spoil their smooth, pleasing contours by digging a huge ravine. He flung a shovelful of earth out to sea, where it formed the islands of Steep Holm and Flat Holm in

Cheddar Gorge is a geological showcase on a dazzling scale.

the Bristol Channel; he carried off the next load to make hills at nearby Brent Knoll and Combwich, and local people used to claim that his hoofmarks could still be seen there.

In the late 1800s, two pioneering explorers of the Cheddar caves were George Cox and his nephew Richard Cox Gough, who gave their names to Cox's Cave and Gough's Cave respectively. They opened the caves to the public and attracted so much interest that a concert was held in one of the entrance passages in 1892. Awestruck visitors compared the weird and diverse rock formations to rows of organ pipes, winged archangels, ropes of onions, and turkeys hanging by the legs.

Undeniably the most sensational discovery was a human skeleton, dug up in Gough's Cave in 1903 and now known as Cheddar Man. At the time, the remains were believed to be between 40,000 and 80,000 years old, but carbon dating has since amended this to around 9,000 years; it is nonetheless the oldest near-complete skeleton of *Homo sapiens* ever found in Britain. DNA analysis shows that people carrying a similar genetic 'fingerprint' still live in the local area, and recently scientists have revealed the likelihood that Cheddar Man had dark skin and pale blue or green eyes.

The Cheddar Caves had even earlier human occupants, in the form of Cro-Magnon hunter-gatherers who are thought to have crossed the land-bridge from Europe some 15,000 years ago. They were skilled toolmakers and left behind items carved from ivory and reindeer antler. They also left evidence of cannibalism, comprising cut-marks and teeth-marks on human bones. Three skulls that had been carefully hollowed out to create cups or bowls provoked a wealth of speculation about the beliefs and practices of our distant ancestors.

According to folklore, in the 10th century one of England's kings narrowly avoided adding his own bones to Cheddar's repository of human relics. King Edmund was on horseback, galloping across the Mendips with a pack of hounds that were chasing a fleeing stag. The stag leapt into the gorge out of desperation, and the dogs followed it and fell to their deaths. Out of control, the King's horse carried him wildly towards the gulf. Edmund believed that he was about to

Cheddar Gorge is one of the few places in Britain known to have inspired a location in J.R.R. Tolkien's Middle Earth.

die; his life flashed before him. In those fleeting seconds, he remembered that he had recently quarrelled with Dunstan, a monk from Glastonbury Abbey whom he had appointed one of his ministers; he quickly prayed for forgiveness and vowed to make amends if his life were spared. His horse halted just short of the precipice and he was saved.

Whether or not this story is true, Dunstan was later elevated to become Abbot of Glastonbury, and under Edmund's successors he rose to become Archbishop of Canterbury. After his death he was canonised as a saint.

There is an old tradition that someone left a pail of milk in the Cheddar caves and eventually went back to find it transformed into cheese. No one really knows how long the caves have been used for maturing Cheddar cheese, but it is likely to have been thousands of years: they offer the perfect environment, with high humidity and constant temperatures.

Cheddar Gorge is one of the few places in Britain known to have inspired a location in J.R.R. Tolkien's Middle Earth, the fantasy landscape in his epic trilogy *The Lord of the Rings*. Tolkien first saw the caves while on honeymoon in 1916, and he visited them again in 1940. In *The Two Towers* (1954), they became the glittering caves of Helm's Deep which are described by the dwarf Gimli in rapturous terms as he rides with Gandalf and Legolas towards Isengard. When Legolas, who loves the freedom of the woods, says that he would pay dearly never to have to descend into such caves, Gimli forgives his jest but says that he speaks like a fool: 'And, Legolas, when the torches are kindled and men walk on the sandy floors under the echoing domes, ah! then, Legolas, gems and crystals and veins of precious ore glint in the polished walls; and the light glows through folded marbles, shell-like, translucent as the living hands of Queen Galadriel.'

STONEHENGE

According to the 12th-century chronicler Geoffrey of
Monmouth, a 5th-century king of the Britons named Aurelius
Ambrosius wanted a fitting monument for his compatriots who
had been murdered by the Saxon warrior Hengist. He sent for the
sorcerer Merlin, who advised him to bring over a stone circle
named 'The Giants' Dance' from the mountain of Killaraus in
Ireland. Merlin assured the king that the stones were of an
impressive size and would stand on his chosen spot forever.

Aurelius wanted to know why he needed to send to Ireland for
stones when they were plentiful in Britain. Merlin's response was
that these ones had healing powers: they had been brought from
Africa by giants, who cured themselves of all ills by dousing the
stones in water and then bathing in it. Convinced, Aurelius
gathered 15,000 men and despatched them to Ireland under the
command of his brother, Uther Pendragon.

The people of Ireland were justifiably angry about the theft of
their stone circle. Uther's men vanquished them in battle and set
about digging it up. However, their tools proved useless and it was
only with the help of Merlin's magic that they managed to lift the
stones and load them into their ships. Back in Britain, they
re-erected the monument in the place where the fallen Britons lay
buried and the delighted king announced a three-day festival in
celebration.

While Geoffrey's story has a timeless appeal, it doesn't contain
a great deal of historical fact. Stonehenge actually began its life
around 3000 BC, long before the arrival of the Anglo-Saxons in

the 5th century AD. The first monument comprised a bank and ditch encircling a ring of pits – the sockets, perhaps, for wooden posts – many of which contained cremated human remains. Around 2500 BC the enormous sarsen* stones and the smaller bluestones were erected, in a supreme feat of logistics and manpower.

While the sarsen stones were hewn from the nearby Marlborough Downs, the bluestones were transported all the way from the Preseli Hills in south-west Wales. Research has suggested that the bluestones may originally have stood in a circle at Waun Mawn, close to the quarry site, and that this circle was later

* Sarsen may derive from an Anglo-Saxon word meaning 'a troublesome stone'. An alternative explanation suggests it comes from 'Saracen', which in medieval times described Arab Muslims, and evolved into an adjective denoting 'non-Christian'.

dismantled and taken to Stonehenge. If this is the case, it makes an interesting echo of the story about The Giants' Dance.

What went on at Stonehenge in Wiltshire? While we can only speculate, archaeology has yielded some clues. At nearby Durrington Walls, which may have been an encampment of Stonehenge's builders, the discarded bones of cattle and pigs suggest large-scale feasting; if the animals were born in spring, their age points to a midwinter gathering. Stonehenge itself is aligned on the midwinter sunset: from the centre of the circle, the sun appears to sink between the two uprights of the tallest trilithon* and to set directly above the Altar Stone (which is now obscured by a fallen sarsen). The changing seasons were of huge

* Two vertical megaliths supporting a stone lintel.

importance to early farmers and herders, who may have gathered to witness the solstice or 'standing still' of the sun, and to be reassured by its subsequent movement northwards.

In the opposite direction, at midsummer the rising sun skims one edge of the outlying Heel Stone (which may once have had a twin, so that the sun appeared between them), and pierces the open 'horseshoe' of trilithons. This phenomenon still draws hundreds of pilgrims to Stonehenge every year, hoping (as its builders must surely have done) that the fickle British weather will bless them with a clear sky at the crucial moment.

From the stone circle, a banked avenue leads to the River Avon.

Studies have suggested that the monument, when complete, acted as a kind of sound chamber, amplifying music and speech.

Underlying the avenue are parallel stripes of ridges and gullies, formed during the Ice Age, and they happen to be precisely aligned on the axis of midwinter sunset and midsummer sunrise. Maybe this is what drew people here in the first place: natural landmarks, inspiring perhaps the most iconic man-made landmark of them all.

Early visitors to Stonehenge included the antiquarian John Aubrey, who first noticed the ring of pits that are now called 'Aubrey Holes' in his honour, as well as the diarist Samuel Pepys and the artists John Constable and J.M.W. Turner. By the late 19th century, tourists were arriving in horse-drawn wagons, but it was still possible to experience Stonehenge in solitude.

On a hot, still day in August 1875, the clergyman Francis Kilvert walked across Salisbury Plain, inhaling the scents of heather and thyme and watching wheatears flicker along the dusty track. He could see the great monument of Stonehenge many miles away in the hazy distance, and was awestruck when he drew closer. In his diary he wrote: 'As I entered the charmed circle of the sombre Stones I instinctively uncovered my head. It was like entering a great Cathedral Church.' (*Kilvert's Diary*, 1940.)

To Tess Durbeyfield and her husband Angel Clare, fleeing across Wessex in Thomas Hardy's *Tess of the d'Urbervilles* (1891), Stonehenge is a pagan temple. On a moonless night the stones loom up suddenly across their path and they have to feel their way around them in the dark, sensing their immense size only from the deeper blackness where they blot out the sky. Tess notices an intriguing phenomenon: '"It hums," said she. "Hearken!" He listened. The wind, playing upon the edifice, produced a booming tune like the note of some gigantic one-stringed harp.'

Hardy knew Stonehenge well and in windy conditions he had heard it generating a strange musical hum. In *The Trumpet Major* (1880), he describes 'the night-wind blowing through Simon Burden's few teeth as through the ruins of Stonehenge'. Perhaps he had a point: studies have suggested that the monument, when complete, acted as a kind of sound chamber, amplifying music and speech. Although this isn't believed to be a deliberate design feature, it is intriguing to imagine how Neolithic people might have created their own soundscape within the circle, using human voices and the music of drums, horns and pipes.

SILBURY HILL

Rising from the flood plain of the River Kennet, Silbury Hill in Wiltshire is a pleasing cone of earth with a flattened top, like a giant prehistoric pudding that has been turned out of a wide-brimmed basin. From the adjacent A4, which follows the route of a Roman road, it immediately catches the eye. Questions arise: How old is it? Why was it built? What lies beneath?

We can really only answer one of these questions. Silbury is believed to have been built between 2470 and 2350 BC, placing it in the late Neolithic period. Its purpose, however, has baffled generations of historians and archaeologists. Writing in 1670, the Wiltshire-born antiquary John Aubrey added a fragment of folklore: 'No History gives us any account of it: the tradition only is, that King Sil, or Zel as the countrey folke pronounce, was buried here on horseback, and that the hill was raysed whilst a posset of milk was seething.' (*Wiltshire: The Topographical Collections of John Aubrey, 1659–70*, ed. J.E. Jackson, 1862.)

Convinced that an ancient burial lay at its heart, in 1776 Colonel Edward Drax and a group of miners sank a vertical shaft into the hill. No sign of burial was discovered. In 1849, John Merewether, Dean of Hereford, oversaw the burrowing of a horizontal tunnel, with the same disappointing result. Then, between 1968 and 1970, a team led by Professor Richard Atkinson dug another tunnel; their conclusion was that the hill had been constructed in phases – Atkinson described it as a 'biological sandwich' – but they failed to find a grave.

Unfortunately, none of these tunnels was properly back-filled and in 2000 a crater opened up on the summit, prompting a programme of emergency restoration in which the cavities were carefully surveyed and then refilled with chalk.

Archaeologists now know a little more about how the hill was built. A layer of topsoil and stones was stripped from the ground, and a small mound was raised, perhaps using gravel from the River Kennet. Over time – maybe a handful of generations – it rose to a height of 102 feet (31 metres) and expanded to cover 5 acres (2 hectares) of land. This is the largest artificial prehistoric mound in Europe, made even more extraordinary by the concept of its builders using antler picks as tools.

Surrounding the hill is a wide ditch that regularly fills with floodwater, and this gives Silbury an additional dimension. Freshly built, with its glistening chalk slopes rising from a reflective pool of water, it must have made an impressive sight. In *Secret Britain* (2020), anthropologist Mary-Ann Ochota notes that Silbury lies on a confluence of springs and seasonal streams, which flow into the Kennet and ultimately into the Thames; she explains that the sources of important rivers are revered in many cultures across the world, and suggests that for its Neolithic builders, Silbury Hill may have marked a sacred place.

Stories of a long-lost king still linger like shreds of morning mist.

Despite the absence of human remains, stories of a long-lost king still linger like shreds of morning mist. He is said to be buried in golden armour, while another story has him lying in a golden coffin. On moonlit nights, he is supposed to gallop around the hill.

Another local legend tells how Silbury Hill was formed. The townspeople of Marlborough and Devizes were always coming to blows, so the folks from Marlborough asked the Devil to settle the dispute by dropping a hill on their enemies. But Saint John overheard and warned the people of Devizes, who sent out their oldest resident, a wily veteran, with a sackful of old boots. The Devil met him en route and asked him how far it was to Devizes; the old man replied that he would never get there that night, or for many nights thereafter, as he himself had left Devizes when he was a youth and had worn out all the boots he was carrying. In annoyance, the Devil threw down the hill where he stood and stormed off. It would make a perfect epilogue if some future investigation were to reveal the burial of an old man with an assortment of footwear.

While we continue to wonder what – if anything – lies beneath Silbury Hill, poets have offered their own speculations about its contents. Robert Southey believed that it was 'Rear'd o'er a Chieftain of the Age of Hills ... whose gallant deeds / Haply at many a solemn festival / The Scald* hath sung ....' ('For a Tablet at Silbury-hill', *The Poetical Works of Robert Southey*, 1847.)

In 1849 Emmeline Fisher, a second cousin of William Wordsworth, composed a poem which was placed in an urn and left in one of the excavation tunnels made by John Merewether. With sensitivity, she regrets the disturbance and expresses a wish that must surely be echoed by all visitors, past and present:

---

* A 'scald' or 'skald' was a poet in the Old Norse tradition.

Bones of our wild forefathers, O forgive,
If we now pierce the chambers of your rest,
And open your dark pillows to the eye
Of the irreverent Day! Hark, as we move,
Runs no stern whisper through the narrow vault?
Flickers no shape across our torch-light pale,
With backward beckoning arm? No, all is still.
O that it were not! O that sound or sign,
Vision or legend, or the eagle glance
Of science, could call back thy history lost,
Green Pyramid of the Plains, from far-ebbed Time!

('Lines on the Opening of Silbury Hill',
3 August 1849)

The urn containing the poem was retrieved by Professor Atkinson during the 1960s.

AVEBURY

Where Kennet rises with a pregnant Rill
And glides thro fatt'ning Meads serenely still
Old Avebury's Relicks feed the curious Eye
And great in Ruins Roman Structures lie.

(Samuel Bowden, *Antiquities and Curiosities
in Wiltshire and Somerset*, 1733)

The seventh of January 1649. England was in the throes of Civil
War. King Charles I, who had been held in captivity for several
months, was being tried for treason. Temporarily forgetting about
the turbulence of anarchy, a young student of Trinity College,
Oxford set out on an exhilarating cross-country hunt with his
friends, all of them staunch Royalists. In breathless pursuit of the
hounds, he galloped into a village near Marlborough in Wiltshire
and what he saw stopped him completely in his tracks.

It wasn't as if Avebury was hard to miss. The largest prehistoric
stone circle in the world, it has a village built within its 0.8-mile
(1.3-km) circumference; its truly gargantuan megaliths include
the heaviest standing stone in the British Isles (the back-stone of
the Cove, which weighs 100 tonnes). It was merely waiting for
someone with a passion for antiquities to fully appreciate its scale
and significance, and that person was John Aubrey.

Aubrey, who has been called England's first archaeologist,
neglected the hunt as he wandered in awe around the henge and
its smaller circles and avenues. He wrote that Avebury 'did as

much exceed in greatness the so renowned Stonehenge as a cathedral doeth a parish church'. (John Britton, *Memoir of John Aubrey*, 1845.) It was, Aubrey suggested, the work of the Druids: at that time, these mysterious 'priests', mentioned in the 1st-century writings of Pliny the Elder, were believed to have constructed temples for pagan worship.

Aubrey survived the Civil War, and after the Restoration he was able to show Avebury to a very interested King Charles II. He produced the first plan of Avebury's henge and circles in his *Monumenta Britannica* (1665–93), but felt obliged to explain the curious similarity between his own name and the old spelling of Avebury as *Aubury*: 'But here, methinkes, I see some Reader smile to himself, thinkinge how I have strained the Place to be of my own Name: not needing that there is a letter's difference, which quite alters the signification of the words.'

In the 1700s another famous antiquary, William Stukeley, upheld Aubrey's theory and took it a stage further. Looking at the Great Henge and its two long avenues of stones leading to Beckhampton and the Sanctuary on Overton Hill, he was convinced that 'the whole figure represented a snake transmitted thro' a circle', and added that 'this is an

Its truly gargantuan megaliths include the heaviest standing stone in the British Isles.

hieroglyphic or symbol of highest note and antiquity'. He even discovered some local folklore to back it up: 'For they say, that in all this trail of ground, which we may call the sacred field, there never was a snake seen; and if a snake should be brought hither, it would not live.' (*Abury, A Temple of British Druids*, 1743.) Among those writers influenced by Stukeley was William Blake, whose epic poem *Jerusalem: The Emanation of the Giant Albion* (1820) described Blake's view of the fall of Albion and featured 'serpent temples'.

The outer circle once comprised around 100 standing stones.

Although Stukeley's ideas were fanciful, his records preserve an appalling account of how Avebury's stones were being broken up for building material. Local people would dig a pit next to the stone, topple it in, pile straw all around and set light to it, and then, while the stone was still scorching hot, they would pour cold water over it until it cracked and split. Stukeley claimed that he 'could easily trace the obit [obituary] of every stone; who did it, for what purpose, and when, and by what method, what house or wall was built out of it, and the like'. (*Abury, A Temple of British Druids*, 1743.)

This wasn't even the first instance of wanton destruction at Avebury. Between the 14th and 18th centuries, motivated perhaps by antagonism towards pagan beliefs or a more practical urge to clear space for cultivation, local people dug enormous holes and buried some of the stones. Many were unearthed and restored in the 1930s, and during the excavations a skeleton of an unfortunate man – thought by his tools to be a barber-surgeon – was found beneath one of them. He had probably been helping to enlarge the hole when the stone – now called the Barber's Stone – had fallen on him.

It is believed that the outer circle once comprised around 100 standing stones, of which only 30 survive. When it was built, which was between 2850 and 2200 BC, it must have made a breathtaking sight, ringed by a bank rising to nearly 55 feet (17 metres) above a 30-foot (9-metre) ditch, and flanked by two magnificent avenues of standing stones. Who walked between them and what were they going to do? Without travelling back in time, we can only speculate.

During the First World War, a Wiltshire-born writer wondered whether she had done exactly that. Edith Maud Olivier, a rector's daughter who was overseeing the Women's Land Army, was

driving through Avebury when she found herself on a road that she didn't recognise: rows of huge grey megaliths loomed on either side through curtains of soft rain. She got out of the car and climbed the bank of the henge, where she could see a village fair in full swing. As the rain worsened, Edith retreated to her car and thought no more of it until a few years later, when she returned to Avebury and learned that no fairs had been held there since 1850. Even more fascinating was the discovery that her row of megaliths did not exist: she had seemingly driven down a 'ghost avenue' from Avebury's Neolithic past.

TORBARROW

It sounds like a scene from an Indiana Jones film. Two labourers, digging at the foot of a hill, accidentally break through into an old tunnel. They follow it and find a cavern full of treasure, but it is guarded by a terrifying armed warrior who strikes at them when they approach.

The setting for this drama is a man-made mound named Torbarrow, which lies on the outskirts of Cirencester in Gloucestershire. It is quite modest in size, being about 10 feet (3 metres) high, and covered with mature trees. It doesn't exactly look like the Temple of Doom.

But a fantastic story was in circulation in 1685, thanks to a broadsheet printed at Fleet Bridge, London. Beginning with the headline of 'A strange and wonderful discovery newly made of

Houses Under Ground, at Colton's-Field in Gloucestershire', it recounts the adventure at great length.

The two workmen were digging a gravel pit when they noticed some loose ground in the side of their trench. They picked away at it and revealed an entrance to a tunnel that appeared to lead into the heart of the hill. They ventured down it and came into a musty chamber that was furnished with long tables and benches; when they touched them, they crumbled into dust. A passage led away into a kitchen with rusting pots and kettles, and then to a parlour whose carpet disintegrated at their step.

Then they entered a room which they assumed to be a place of worship, from the images and ornate carvings on the wall; they noticed urns filled with gold and silver coins that bore the heads of Roman emperors. They tried their strength against a closed wooden door and were horrified when it fell away to reveal the full-size 'image' of a man, apparently alive and wielding a club; he was brilliantly lit by a burning lamp and he struck out when one of them dared to approach.

'A strange and wonderful discovery newly made of Houses Under Ground.'

Taking to their heels in terror, the men fled back outside and sought the help of a local antiquarian. This gentleman was impressed with the handful of coins that they'd picked up and agreed to go back with them the next day to investigate. Together they re-entered the mound, passed through the antechambers and arrived at the doorway with the fierce warrior. The antiquarian believed that it was some kind of automaton and was undeterred by its threatening posture; as he stepped through, the figure dealt a blow and shattered the glass lamp which was lighting the cave, plunging it into darkness. Luckily, the three men had brought their own lantern and candles.

They inspected the warrior and found him to be the effigy of a Roman general. Next to him lay two severed and embalmed human heads with tresses of long, flowing hair. The would-be archaeologists were looking for further tunnels when they were startled by a deep groaning noise, which seemed to fill the chamber. Sensing imminent disaster, they raced back into the daylight and turned to see the mound collapsing. Everything was now buried, apart from the coins they had salvaged the previous day.

> *The would-be archaeologists were looking for further tunnels when they were startled by a deep groaning noise.*

Sadly, historians have since dismissed the whole story as pure fabrication. The protagonists were not named and none of their purported treasure seems to have survived. The story did, however, attract the interest of antiquary John Aubrey, who kept a copy of the broadsheet in his records about ancient sites. Aubrey had noted another mysterious account of Torbarrow: 'Anno, 1670, not far from Cirencester was an apparition: being demanded, whether a good spirit or a bad? returned no answer, but disappeared with a curious perfume and a most melodious twang.' (*Miscellanies*, 1696.)

In the late 1700s, the antiquarian William Stukeley revealed that several Roman coins had been dug up from the mound and that a ploughman had found a lidded stone coffin with the remains of a body in it in a nearby field. An amateur excavation of the mound took place in the 19th century, which yielded only fragments of pottery, thought at the time to be pre-Roman.

The current interpretation of Torbarrow (also known as Tar Barrow, or by its older name of Starbury) is that it is a prehistoric or pre-Roman round barrow (burial mound); a second barrow is located about 220 yards (200 metres) away. Close by are the buried remains of a Romano-British funerary and ritual site.

In folklore, barrows have long been associated with hauntings. It is a familiar belief that the spirits of the dead tend to linger close to their physical remains, but a guardian of tomb treasure seems to have had a special identity. Writing about the Norse sagas, the folklorist Andrew Lang observed that 'in the graves where treasures were hoarded the Barrowwights dwelt, ghosts that were sentinels over the gold'. ('The Sagas', from *Essays in Little*, 1891.) In J.R.R. Tolkien's *The Lord of the Rings* trilogy, a barrow-wight is a dark phantom with luminous eyes that protects the ancient burial grounds of Middle Earth.

So, even if the labourers and the gold never existed, a barrow-wight might – just conceivably – still be lingering in the depths of Torbarrow, ready to attack anyone who is foolish enough to disturb its contents.

SOUTH EAST ENGLAND

CHANCTONBURY RING

Tramping the Sussex Downs on a long-distance summer walk, the author Robert Macfarlane bedded down for the night amid the trees of Chanctonbury Ring. Around two in the morning he was woken by a human-like scream coming from the other side of the copse. As he listened, another voice started shrieking; the two sounds started to move around the Ring, in different directions but drawing ever closer to where he lay.

Writing in his book *The Old Ways* (2012), Macfarlane explains that he was unaware of Chanctonbury's reputation at the time. It was only when he went home and read about the place that he found he was not the first person to have an unsettling experience there. In 1966 a group of bikers fled in terror from a series of wails that began at midnight and seemed to move around the trees.

Owls, perhaps? A rabbit caught by a fox? Both can produce alarming noises ... but there are other stories. Some visitors have had an eerie sensation of being followed; one person felt chilled, with a sudden sense of impending doom. In 1936 Dr Philip Gosse, who lived in nearby Steyning, decided to visit the Ring at night with his wife; he did not reveal what happened but vowed never to go back.

> *Around two in the morning he was woken by a human-like scream coming from the other side of the copse.*

Chanctonbury Ring is one of the many enclosures and hill forts that sprinkle the undulating chalk landscape of the South Downs.

Encompassing an area of about 3½ acres (1.4 hectares) on top of Chanctonbury Hill, it is roughly oval in shape and was constructed by earth being thrown inwards to create a high bank and an encircling ditch. The resulting Ring has been dated to the late Bronze Age, but archaeological evidence suggests that it was occupied only intermittently, and abandoned around the mid-4th century BC.

Five hundred years later, the Romans built two temples within the Ring, the only traces of which are now below ground. Archaeological finds, including bones from the heads and jaws of pigs, have led to suggestions of ritual use, perhaps extending further back than the Roman period. Local landowner Sir Charles Goring planted the hilltop trees in 1760, and over the centuries the distinctive clump became a much-loved landmark. When it was devastated by the Great Storm of 1987, some emergency archaeological work was carried out before the hill was replanted.

It has been suggested that a distant memory of arcane practices is preserved in the folklore of Chanctonbury. According to tradition, if you walk (or run) seven times around the Ring – at midnight, or on a moonless night, or at seven in the morning on Midsummer's Day – the Devil is supposed to come out of the wood and hand you a basin of soup (or milk, or porridge, depending on the version of the tale). Writing in the *Folklore* journal ('Legends of Chanctonbury Ring', 1969), Jacqueline Simpson wonders whether these foods were once offered as ritual drinks in a Romano-Celtic temple.

Another story claims that the number of trees on the hill can never be counted, for fear of raising the ghosts of Julius Caesar and his armies. Campers have heard the galloping of horses' hoofs, and one picnicker was astonished to see a white-robed druid emerge from the mist. The ghost of an old bearded man, reported in the 19th century, was assumed to be seeking a hoard of Anglo-Saxon coins dug up on a nearby farm in 1866. The writer R.D. Blackmore describes this figure in his novel *Alice Lorraine* (1875), and claims that, now that the treasure has been found, 'the spectral owner roves no more'. However, the ghost was apparently still doing some roving in the 1940s and was seen so often that local people were afraid to go up to the Ring for fear of encountering him.

Balancing these mysteries are the thousands of people who visit Chanctonbury for its beauty. Virginia Woolf wrote that the South Downs were 'enough to float a whole population in happiness, if only they would look'. (*A Writer's Diary*, 1953.) From the hilltop there are far-reaching views across the downland towards the south coast; green woodpecker, nuthatch and nightingale have been recorded in the woods, while chalkhill blue butterflies dance above the surrounding fields.

If you walk seven times around the Ring the Devil is supposed to come out of the wood and hand you a basin of soup.

The writer and broadcaster S.P.B. Mais organised a special public excursion to Chanctonbury on 17 July 1932. A passionate advocate of country walking, he had advertised the event around London and was expecting a few dozen people to board the midnight train at Victoria Station. But well over a thousand people turned up, among them bowler-hatted businessmen, and they all climbed the hill to watch the sunrise. In the years that followed, countryside railway excursions became increasingly popular.

In 1915 the memory of Chanctonbury inspired a moving poem by John Stanley Purvis, as he contemplated the trenches of the Great War:

> I can't forget the lane that goes from Steyning to the Ring
> In summer time, and on the downs how larks and linnets
> sing
> High in the sun. The wind comes off the sea, and oh, the
> air!
> I never knew till now that life in old days was so fair.
> But now I know it in this filthy rat-infested ditch,
> Where every shell must kill or spare, and God alone knows
> which.
> And I am made a beast of prey, and this trench is my lair –
> My God, I never knew till now that those days were so fair,
> And we assault in half-an-hour, and it's a silly thing:
> I can't forget the lane that goes from Steyning to the Ring.

(2nd Lt John Stanley Purvis, writing as
Philip Johnson, 'Chance Memory', *Daily News*, 1916;
incidentally, Purvis did survive the war)

THE WHITE CLIFFS OF DOVER

There is a cliff, whose high and bending head
Looks fearfully in the confined deep.
Bring me but to the very brim of it …

(The Earl of Gloucester, from Shakespeare's
King Lear, Act IV, Sc. I, c. 1606)

At the beginning of his book *In Search of England* (1927), the travel writer H.V. Morton remembers a time when he was in the Middle East and believed himself to be dying. Grieving for his home country of England, he vowed that if he lived to see Kent's White Cliffs of Dover again, he would never leave them.

Morton did survive and on his return he celebrated his love of England by embarking on a whimsical tour of the entire country. The point is that for Morton, and for generations of people like him who sailed across the English Channel to continental Europe, the White Cliffs were the last view they had of Britain's shores, and they represented everything that was dear to them about their homeland. The song '(There'll be Bluebirds Over) The White Cliffs of Dover', by Walter Kent and Nat Burton, and sung by Vera Lynn, expresses the yearning felt by servicemen and women who were stationed abroad during the Second World War.

Throughout history, the White Cliffs have been seen as a symbol of intrinsic Britishness, offering either a warning or a welcome to visitors from across the sea. For Julius Caesar and his legions, scouting the coast from their galleys in 55 BC, they served as a natural deterrent, blocking any route inland. Further discouragement was offered by lines of fierce-looking Britons who had gathered on the clifftops, ready to hurl missiles on any Romans unwise enough to step ashore.

In AD 46, after their invasion of Britain, the Romans built two lighthouses on the cliffs, their burning braziers helping to guide vessels safely into Portus Dubris, the Roman port of Dover. One of these lighthouses still stands and is one of only three such buildings to survive from the Roman Empire (the others are in Spain and Libya).

Also sitting atop the cliffs is Dover Castle, an impressive 12th-century fortress which may occupy the site of an Iron Age hill fort. Beneath its ramparts, defensive tunnels were burrowed into the cliffs in the early 13th century, making the castle more capable of withstanding a siege, and this underground network was expanded in the early 1800s when Napoleon's rise to power made the threat of French invasion very real.

The tunnels were used as a military hospital during the First and Second World Wars, and it was from here that the evacuation of British troops from Dunkirk – code-named 'Operation Dynamo' – was masterminded in May 1940. More tunnels were excavated on the orders of Prime Minister Winston Churchill in November 1940, resulting in the formidable Fan Bay gun battery, which helped protect the Channel against enemy shipping.

Geologically speaking, the White Cliffs owe their brilliance to a white mud that was formed around 70 million years ago, when this part of Britain was submerged under a shallow sea. Fragments of coccoliths – tiny plates of calcium carbonate formed by single-celled algae – were deposited as sediment, along with larger organisms such as sponges and sea urchins. Later, this seabed was lifted upwards by tectonic forces, and the cliffs were shaped by the erosive action of ice sheets during the last glacial period.

Legend offers an entirely different explanation. The White Cliffs, so it is said, owe their existence to a gigantic mythical ship

called *The Merry Dun of Dover*, and her story was told not just in England but in the Friesian Islands (an archipelago off the coast of the Netherlands, Germany and Denmark) and in Scandinavia. In the Friesian Islands she was called the *Mannigfual* and her captain was Wêda, the Friesian version of the Norse god Odin.

The Merry Dun was so big that her captain, mounted on horseback, took six weeks to ride from bow to stern. She had a thousand beds, each holding a thousand men, and young boys who climbed up the masts came down as old men with grey beards. Because of her size she sailed only in the deepest parts of the ocean and the sound of thunder was interpreted as the billowing of her sails.

Many thousands of years ago, when there was still dry land between England and France, *The Merry Dun* sailed into the North Sea in thick fog and found that she was too big to turn around. Seeing land looming ahead, the captain commanded his crew to soap the ship's sides. They got to work quickly and she sliced her way through, creating the cliffs of Dover which remained coated with a thick layer of white soap. The sea surged in her wake, pouring into the passage which became the English Channel. As she passed by, her sails swept a flock of sheep from Dover into the sea and toppled a church steeple in Calais.

During her voyages around the world's oceans, *The Merry Dun* encountered gigantic fish and sea monsters; eventually she was raised into the heavens, to be crewed by the gods. During violent storms she is still said to sail across the sky, emitting lightning bolts from her captain's pipe.

ROLLRIGHT STONES

Long ago, a legendary king set out to conquer England. As he and his warriors marched across the Cotswolds, they were hailed by a witch who knew all about their plans. She issued a challenge to the king:

> Seven long strides shalt thou take,
> And if Long Compton thou canst see
> King of England thou shalt be!

Knowing that the Warwickshire village of Long Compton was easily visible, the king replied:

> Stick, stock, stone,
> As King of England I shall be known.

He took seven strides, but was dismayed to see a mound of earth rise in front of him, obscuring the village from view. The witch was triumphant, and declared:

> As Long Compton thou canst not see
> King of England thou shalt not be;
> Rise up stick and stand still stone,
> For King of England thou shalt be none;
> Thou and thy men stones shall be,
> And I myself an eldern-tree.

As she spoke, the king and his men turned into stone: the warriors formed a circle, known as the King's Men, while the king was transformed into the King Stone. A group of followers, who were huddled together and quietly plotting the king's downfall, suffered the same fate and became the Whispering Knights. The witch, as promised, vanished into an elder tree, and folklore claims that it still grows nearby, keeping watch over the petrified warriors to make sure the spell isn't broken.

The stones of this age-old legend can be seen today, in fields either side of a road that runs between the villages of Great Rollright and Little Rollright. They have been created from natural boulders of local Jurassic limestone, and have weathered into strange shapes with a surface that is pitted and pierced with holes. In the 1700s, William Stukeley described them as being 'corroded like wormeaten wood by the harsh Jaws of Time'. (*Palaeographia Britannica*, 1743.)

Carbon dating has revealed a difference of about a thousand years between each grouping: the King Stone, which marks a Bronze Age cemetery, has been dated to about 1500 BC, while the King's Men stone circle is thought to have been created about 2500 BC, in the late Neolithic period. The Whispering Knights is an early Neolithic dolmen (megalithic tomb), dating from about 3500 BC.

The stones are so characterful that it isn't hard to imagine the fairies that are said to dwell beneath them. Writing in 1895, the archaeologist Arthur J. Evans recorded the story of a local man, Will Hughes, who had seen fairies dancing around the King Stone at night. Will's wife, Betsy, remembered that they came out of a hole in the bank, and added that when she was a girl she and her friends would put a rock over it to keep them in, but that they always found it turned over the next morning.

The stones' weird shapes are not entirely due to the weather. In an old tradition, practised even in the 19th century, visitors would chip small pieces off the King Stone as lucky charms. Welsh drovers, passing by with their herds of cattle on the way to market, took a piece to ensure a safe journey, and soldiers would carry a fragment onto the battlefield, believing that it offered protection.

There are distant folk memories of midsummer festivities held on an oblong strip of ground near the King Stone. On a fine evening around harvest-time, local girls would put their ears to the stones of the Whispering Knights in the belief that they would hear a prediction about their future. At midnight, all of the stones were said to go down to drink at a spring in Little Rollright Spinney – people would point to gaps in the bushes where they pushed through – while another tale said that they came alive and danced in a circle.

There is an enduring superstition, also found at other sites in Britain, that it is impossible to count all the stones of the circle and get the same answer twice. A baker tried to do it by putting a loaf on every stone, but when he collected them he found that some were missing, no doubt spirited away by hungry fairies.

Folk tales warn about dire repercussions if a stone is removed. A farmer dragged one away to make a bridge, but 24 horses were needed to move it and a man was killed in the endeavour. The stone was put across the stream, but next morning it was found flipped over onto the bank. In the ensuing weeks the farmer's crops failed and he was haunted by eerie sounds, so he saw no option but to put the stone back; needless to say, all his torments then stopped.

In 2015, an intriguing 7th-century burial was discovered close to the King Stone: a Saxon woman, about 25 to 30 years of age, with no indication of the cause of death. Her grave goods were described by archaeologists as 'amuletic'. They included a faceted bead of rock crystal, a disc made of deer antler, and a long-handled bronze skillet or *trulleum*. In *Secret Britain* (2020), Mary-Ann Ochota explains that the *trulleum* is an item more commonly associated with the Byzantine empire, and was used in hand-washing rituals; it was obviously a precious artefact, as it had been placed in a lockable wooden casket.

It is tempting to see in this enigmatic Saxon woman some kind of magical association or ability, like the witch in the legend. What did she do here, and why? We can only imagine.

WAYLAND'S SMITHY

'Where are now the bones of that famous and wise goldsmith Weland? ... Where are the bones of Weland now, and who knows now where they may be?'

(King Alfred, Old English version of *Boethius: de Consolatione Philosophiae*, ed. W.J. Sedgefield, 1899)

Close to the village of Ashbury in Oxfordshire, and about a mile south-west of the Uffington White Horse on the old track of the Ridgeway, is a chambered long barrow curiously named Wayland's Smithy. Dating from the Neolithic period, between 3460 and

3400 BC, it consists of a mound of earth about 60 yards (55 metres) long, trapezoidal in shape, covering a burial chamber that once held the remains of several people.

Four huge sarsen stones (originally six) guard the entrance and smaller stones mark out the perimeter. Amazingly, this structure overlies another barrow, some 150 years older, which was deliberately sealed after a very short period of use. Fourteen people had been laid to rest there, including two women and a child.

Although Wayland's Smithy lies in an open landscape of farmland, it is ringed by beech trees which shelter it from the outside world. On a winter's evening, with mist moving like a cold breath between the stones, it's easy to imagine that the old spirits still walk here. Even in relatively recent times, children tiptoed up to the chamber and listened for the clink of a smith's hammer; so too did their ancestors, stretching back in an unbroken line for a thousand years, to the time of the Anglo-Saxons. King Alfred himself knew the tale and versions of it were told in feasting halls across Northern Europe.

Weland or Wayland was the smith's name, but the Norsemen knew him as Völundr. He was a supernatural being – either a giant or an elf – and an Old Norse poem, *Völundarkviða* ('The lay of Völundr'), tells how he and his two brothers came upon three swan-maidens by a lake, and lived with them for seven years before the swan-maidens flew away. The brothers moved on but Völundr stayed and learned the craft of metalworking, making beautiful gold rings to give his wife in case she returned.

Völundr's skill was coveted by King Niðhad (or Nithuthr), who captured him, stole his rings, cut his hamstrings to stop him from fleeing and forced him to craft more gold for his own benefit. Plotting revenge, Völundr waited until the king's two sons visited him and killed them both, lining their skulls with gold and presenting them to his master. Still not satisfied, when the king's daughter, Böðvildr (or Beadohild), came to him, asking him to mend a gold ring (one which Völundr himself had made for his wife), he forced himself upon her, made her pregnant and then flew away on wings that he had fashioned for himself, mocking the king loudly as he did so.

The art of smithing has long been associated with magic. To our forebears, the use of fire to draw metal from stone and work it into fine objects must have seemed akin to sorcery: think of Excalibur, possibly the most famous sword of all, wielded in battle by King Arthur. Geoffrey of Monmouth's *Vita Merlini* (c. 1150) alludes to a goblet made by Guielandus (Weland), and in Anglo-Saxon poetry the term 'the work of Weland' was a byword for weapons of extraordinary quality. In the Old English epic poem *Beowulf*, when the eponymous hero arrives at the hall of King Hrothgar and prepares to fight the monster, Grendel, he declares:

> If I fall in the battle,
> Send to Higelac the armour that serveth
> To shield my bosom, the best of equipments,
> Richest of ring-mails; 'tis the relic of Hrethla,
> The work of Wayland.

> (*Beowulf*, trans. John Lesslie Hall, 1892)

While smiths provided a valuable service to humans, they dwelt in the dark recesses of the earth – in Wayland's case, the barrow's chamber – and had one foot in the Otherworld. This duality is reflected in Wayland's nature, which at first is patient and loving, but later vengeful and barbaric. Among the scenes that appear on the beautifully carved 8th-century box known as the Franks Casket, held in the British Museum, is an image that shows Wayland at his forge, holding a human head in his tongs.

There is a long-standing local tradition that if a traveller's horse has lost a shoe they have only to tether the animal overnight at Wayland's Smithy, leaving a silver sixpence nearby, and in the morning they will find it newly shod and the money gone. And every hundred years, the chalk figure of the

The art of smithing has long been associated with magic.

Uffington White Horse is said to gallop over from its hilltop paddock, to be reshod by Wayland the blacksmith.

The place name of Wayland's Smithy can be traced back at least as far as a 10th-century charter, when it was referred to as Welandes smiððe. But has any metalworking ever been done here? The legendary occupant is unlikely to emerge from the bowels of the earth and tell us the answer, but in the early 1900s two iron 'currency bars' (or possibly unfinished swords) dating from the Iron Age were dug up – offerings, perhaps, to the invisible giant who conjured metal out of fire.

THE WHITE HORSE
OF UFFINGTON

*Gerllaw tref Abinton y mae mynydd ac eilun march
arno a gwyn ydiw. Ni thyf dim arno.*

'Near the town of Abingdon is a mountain with
an image of a stallion on it, and it is white. Nothing
grows on it.'

(*Llyfr Coch Hergest* or 'Red Book of Hergest',
c. 1382–1410)

Incised into a hillside in the chalk downs of Oxfordshire is the
figure of a horse. The creature appears to be running, with its long
tail flowing and its head slightly bowed; its outline looks as if it
has been painted with quick, decisive brushstrokes. Some
anatomical features, including the line of its belly, are left entirely
to the imagination, while others, such as its two short 'tusks' or
extended lips, defy interpretation. It is bold, elegant and
breathtakingly different. Our immediate impression is one of deep
antiquity, of an animal seen through eyes other than our own.

The White Horse is a geoglyph – a design created on the
surface of the Earth – and it measures some 374 feet (114 metres)
in length by about 110 feet (34 metres) in height. The first written
mention of it occurs in a cartulary (a register of privileges) of
Abingdon Abbey, in which a monk named Godric Cild is the
inheritor of land near White Horse Hill around AD 1070.

Curiously, in an early list of the wonders of Britain (*De mirabilibus Britanniae*, c. 1100), it is described as a white horse with its foal. While there is no evidence that a second animal ever existed, an old tradition describes the White Horse as a mare with an invisible foal. At night, so it is said, they come down to graze in the valley known as the Manger, and they drink from Woolstone Wells – a group of springs that flow from their hoof prints.

In the 17th century, historians wondered who had created the White Horse and why. The antiquary John Aubrey believed it was the work of Hengist, a 5th-century Saxon warrior whose battle-standard bore the image of a white horse. Francis Wise, an Oxford academic, was more precise: in 1738 he published a paper arguing that the White Horse commemorated a victory by King Aethelred and his brother, Alfred, over the Danes in AD 871.

In the early 20th century, the artistic style of the White Horse was compared with horses depicted on Iron Age artefacts from southern England and it was tentatively dated to around 100 BC. But in 1994, samples of the deepest and oldest layers of packed chalk were subjected

It is bold, elegant and breathtakingly different.

to a technique called optically stimulated luminescence, which can determine when quartz sediment was last exposed to sunlight. The result was astonishing: the White Horse was created between 1400 and 600 BC. Even in the eyes of King Alfred and Hengist, it would have been unfathomably ancient.

Recent theories suggest that the figure represents a 'Sun Horse', a symbol of a widespread religion that is now lost. Around the same time as the domestication of the horse, which began about 5,500 years ago, a belief was spreading across Asia and Europe that associated the horse with the sky and the sun. The Sun Horse drew the sun across the sky, performing an essential role in the cycle of life.

The surrounding area is rich in prehistoric sites. Passing close by is the Ridgeway, an ancient track that runs across the tops of the hills. This long-distance path must have offered huge advantages to the inhabitants of the valley, not just in terms of movement and trade but also for observation and defence. On the hilltop above the chalk figure is an Iron Age hill fort dating from around 700 BC; maybe its residents saw the White Horse as a spiritual guardian connecting them with their ancestors. About a mile to the south-west is a Neolithic long barrow called Wayland's Smithy. All these places were known and used for centuries, emphasising the significance of this ancient landscape.

In 1677, the topographer Thomas Baskerville was the first to record a centuries-old custom: the 'scouring' or cleaning of the White Horse in order to preserve its pristine appearance. Traditionally, the scouring was done every seven years – usually at midsummer. The 'scourers' indulged in a merry festival, with contests such as horse racing, wrestling, pole-climbing – and cheese-rolling, when a large cheese was chased down the hillside into the Manger and claimed by the person who could catch it.

The author Thomas Hughes was born in Uffington, and in 1859 his interest in local history inspired him to write *The Scouring of the White Horse, or the Long Vacation Ramble of a London Clerk*. The story centres around Richard Easy, who

visits the White Horse and witnesses the festival. Flower-decked booths are selling gingerbread, nuts, apples and ribbons, and there are performances by musicians and acrobats. With the beer flowing freely, Richard hears a traditional song being sung by the party of scourers:

> The owld White Harse wants zettin to rights
> And the Squire hev promised good cheer
> Zo we'll gee un a scrape to kip un in zhape,
> An a'll last for many a year.

The preservation of the White Horse is a central theme in an epic poem by G.K. Chesterton. Blending imagination with contemporary historical belief, it begins with King Alfred hiding from the advancing Danes. As he wanders despairingly around the hills, he notices that the White Horse, a long-abandoned symbol of his homeland, is choked with lichen and weeds. Alfred stages a miraculous comeback in battle and then orders the White Horse to be restored to its former glory. To his loyal followers, he declares:

> And though skies alter and empires melt,
> This word shall still be true:
> If we would have the horse of old,
> Scour ye the horse anew.

(G.K. Chesterton, *The Ballad of the White Horse*, 1911)

Nowadays, the White Horse is regularly 'scoured' by parties of volunteers organised by the National Trust. Working in small sections, they remove weeds and apply fresh pieces of chalk, using a hammer to smash them to the required size. Aerial photography shows that the figure has evolved slightly over the centuries, as a result of soil movement and repeated cutting.

A local belief claims that when King Arthur wakes from his long sleep to save England from peril, the White Horse will rise up and dance on a nearby hilltop called Dragon Hill. But this place name gives rise to another question: is the White Horse really a horse at all? An alternative school of thought sees it as the dragon which was slain by Saint George; believers point to a bare patch of chalk on the hilltop, claiming that this is where its blood was spilt.

In 2004, Terry Pratchett set his fantasy novel *A Hat Full of Sky* amid a landscape of chalk downs. The heroine, Tiffany Aching, glimpses a white horse cut into a valley, noticing that its flowing lines make it appear to be moving. The White Horse of Uffington seems to possess a similar quality – it looks wild and transient, as if it has never been permanently captured.

There may be some magic hidden in the White Horse's location, because it has been described as a kind of 'whispering gallery'. In the 1950s, a local writer named Ralph Whitlock visited the site to inspect some restoration work. According to Whitlock, he witnessed the foreman standing on a hillside a quarter of a mile away, giving instructions to his team while speaking in a normal voice; the foreman's words were heard quite distinctly at the White Horse, despite the intervening distance.

CENTRAL ENGLAND AND EAST ANGLIA

STIPERSTONES

When cloud obscures the top of the Stiperstones and the rain comes down in sheets, the Devil, according to Shropshire folk, is sitting in his Chair. Rising to a height of 1,759 feet (536 metres) near Minsterley in south-west Shropshire, the ridge of this long, heather-covered hill is punctuated with huge, jagged outcrops of quartzite, of which the Devil's Chair is the best known.

In the 1800s, when this area was mined for lead, workmen would occasionally hear an eerie knocking that came from deep within the hill. This, they said, was the sound of Wild Edric, a hero from long ago who was sleeping under the Stiperstones; wherever he knocked, good lodes would always be found. It was believed that sometime in the future he would wake and restore the days of old when the land was prosperous and people were safe.

Wild Edric, also known as Eadric Silvaticus, is not just a legendary hero: he was a real-life Anglo-Saxon landowner who earned his nickname by spearheading a fierce resistance to the Normans after the invasion of 1066. Joining forces with the Welsh kings of Gwynedd and Powys, Edric attacked the Norman-held towns of Hereford and Shrewsbury, but was defeated in 1069 at a battle near Stafford. Afterwards, he reached an agreement with William the Conqueror – local sources emphasise that this was not a submission – and accompanied Norman forces in an attack on Scotland.

It is not known what happened to Edric in later life, but in the 12th century he re-emerged as a legendary figure who had a fairy wife named Godda. Edric encountered Godda while she was dancing with her sisters in the forest of Clun; he was enchanted by her beauty and she consented to marry him on condition that he must never reproach her. She warned him that if he broke his word she would disappear, and he would pine away and die.

One evening, Edric arrived home from hunting to find his wife absent. When she returned, he was angry at her lateness and demanded to know if she had been dancing with her sisters. At his unkind words Godda vanished and none of Edric's pleas could bring her back. He died of grief, as she had foretold.

But that was by no means the end of Edric's story. In Shropshire there were folk who preferred to believe that he was still alive and ready to lead them in battle. He and his wife, along with his train of followers, were said to dwell in the tunnels beneath the Stiperstones. In peacetime they guided miners to the richest ore, but when the country was threatened by invasion they would ride out across the moorland in the direction of the enemy.

> *The smell of brimstone is still said to waft around the Devil's Chair.*

In *Shropshire Folk-lore: A Sheaf of Gleanings* (1883), Charlotte Sophia Burne records the account of a woman who had seen them as a young girl. She was walking with her father near Minsterley when they heard the blast of a horn. Recognising the sound, her father told her to cover her face apart from her eyes, and on no account to speak or she would lose her mind.

A band of phantom riders approached at full gallop, led by

Edric on a white horse. The girl noticed his bright, black eyes and dark curly hair; a green cloak was thrown over his shoulders and his sword hung from a golden belt. Godda had long fair hair and wore a green dress with a dagger at her waist. It was just before the Crimean War and they rode north, indicating conflict with Russia. The girl watched them go in silence; her father told her he had seen them before, when he was a boy, riding south towards France and the Napoleonic Wars.

The story of Edric has echoes of the Wild Hunt, a more widespread folkloric tradition in which a host of spectral riders and hounds thunder across the sky, snatching up lost souls. Less dramatic but just as haunting are the Seven Whistlers, whose plaintive cries are sometimes heard over the Stiperstones. The sound has been ascribed to plovers or curlews; it is said that six birds are perpetually seeking a seventh, and their calls foretell disaster.

As for the rocky outcrops, these are supposed to have been dropped by the Devil when he was coming over from Ireland with an apronful of stones. When he sat down to rest, his apron strings broke, depositing the load far short of its destination (which may have been the Wrekin, a hill to the north). He cursed loudly, and the smell of brimstone is still said to waft around the Devil's Chair. This rock formation does resemble a giant's seat, but folklore warns that if anyone dares to sit in it, the Devil will drum up a violent thunderstorm.

In *The Golden Arrow* (1916) by Shropshire writer Mary Webb, the Devil's Chair looms darkly over the tempestuous love lives of Deborah Arden and Stephen Southernwood. Before they are married, Deborah explains to Stephen that at the midwinter solstice all the ghosts of Shropshire meet at the Devil's Chair in order to choose a king for the year. Later, when she believes that Stephen has forsaken her, she drags all the furniture out of their cottage and burns it:

> Above Lostwithin the fire licked the black night with red, forked tongues until a glare lit the brooding sky. Down in the plain women who were awake late shook with fear and woke some one to keep them company. 'The Devil's Chair's burning,' they whispered. 'Maybe it's the end of the 'orld!'

WINNATS PASS

In the museum at Speedwell Cavern in Derbyshire's Peak District is a leather saddle. It is a side-saddle, designed for a lady, and it is about 250 years old. According to folklore, it once belonged to a woman who was eloping with her lover along a high and isolated track called Winnats Pass. Over the years their story has evolved into a bewildering number of variants, but the ending is always the same: whoever they were, and wherever they were going, they didn't make it through Winnats Pass alive.

Much of the Peak District is characterised by bare hills and plateaux, dropping down to wooded river valleys and flood plains. Dark gritstone hills or 'edges' punctuate the region known as the Dark Peak, while in the White Peak the underlying limestone contains the remains of tiny marine creatures which settled in the mud of a tropical sea some 350 million years ago. Limestone is porous and partially soluble, and some 11,000 years ago, at the end of the last glacial period, torrents of meltwater sculpted tunnels and caves along the course of underground rivers. The steep-sided gorge of Winnats Pass was formed from a collapsed cave system, but some spectacular caves remain intact, such as Speedwell Cavern at the east end of the Pass.

The curious name of Winnats Pass is said to come from 'wind gates' or 'windy gates', referring to the wild weather that travellers encountered once they had passed through one of its entrances and begun to ascend the track – which rises to a height of over 1,300 feet (400 metres) between Castleton and Sparrowpit. It was along this track that an eloping couple, known only as Clara and Allan, were riding one day in 1758. They had spent the night at an inn in Castleton and were heading for the Peak Forest Chapel, where they intended to marry. This private chapel, founded in 1657 by the Countess of Devonshire and dedicated to King Charles the Martyr, had developed a reputation as 'Derbyshire's Gretna Green' because it granted marriage licences without the need for banns or witnesses.

The curious name of Winnats Pass is said to come from 'wind gates' or 'windy gates'.

Allan and Clara were careful to conceal their plans, but a band of five ruffians had overheard their conversation in the tavern and followed them, guessing from their fine clothes that they carried

money. Somewhere in the upper reaches of the Pass they ambushed the couple, stole their money and murdered them in a barn. They hid their bodies in a mineshaft, where they were only discovered 10 years later. Meanwhile the couple's horses were found wandering, four days after the crime, one of them still wearing a lady's saddle.

The five men divided their ill-gotten gains between them, but none of them prospered. One used his money to buy horses, all of which mysteriously died, while another man fell off a precipice and a third was hit by a rock falling from a cliff. Of the remaining two, one took his own life and the other went mad. The story of their crime was known only when the last surviving culprit – whose horses had died – confessed on his deathbed, and local people, especially church ministers, were quick to see the vengeful hand of God in their fate.

The identities of Allan and Clara are still unknown: some versions of the legend, including a local folk song, even name the bridegroom as Henry. However, the names of the murderers were local knowledge. In the 18th century, Castleton was a lead-mining area whose inhabitants were poor, and wayside robbery throughout England was a common occurrence. Additionally, in the years after the Jacobite Rebellion of 1745, the area was known to be a haunt of Jacobite supporters who had fled into the Peak District during Bonnie Prince Charlie's retreat from Derby, and these fugitives were greatly feared. Perhaps for these reasons the men felt that they had a chance of avoiding detection – which, of course, they did, although their sense of guilt seems to have devised its own retribution.

'... lightning flashed on the bloody faces of their fated victims; the thunder re-bellowed in the horrible dell, and the guilty murderers trembled with excessive fear.'

(William Wood, *Tales and Traditions of the High Peak*, 1862)

Derbyshire folklore collector William Wood published a highly dramatised version of the story in his *Tales and Traditions of the High Peak*, suggesting that Clara was an English nobleman's daughter of exceptional beauty and Allan was a gentleman from the south of England. Wood had already serialised the tale in a Buxton newspaper and his melodramatic style thrilled Victorian audiences. However, his words must have caused great offence locally, because in a footnote he took pains to assure his quaking readers that the area was no longer a hotbed of iniquity. Wood's attempt to mollify local opinion did nothing to dissuade a Castleton landlord from ejecting him bodily out of a pub window in 1863.

Today, visitors to Winnats Pass revel in its magnificent scenery and wide-open, sweeping views, with Mam Tor and its impressive Bronze Age hill fort rising to the north. Some might be on the lookout for a wild flower called Derby hawkweed (*Hieracium naviense*) which is unique to this location. The semi-precious mineral Blue John has been mined around Castleton since the 18th century, and it was with this in mind that the crime writer Sir Arthur Conan Doyle penned *The Terror of Blue John Gap* (1910), a short story in which a London doctor ventures into a cavern and encounters a monster from a prehistoric world. In Jane

Austen's *Pride and Prejudice* (1813), Elizabeth Bennet tours the Peak District and has an unexpected encounter with Mr Darcy; it must be said, however, that when the subject of a tour was first broached, Elizabeth was 'excessively disappointed', because she had set her heart on seeing the Lakes!

SHERWOOD FOREST

Lithe and lysten, gentylmen,
That be of frebore blode;
I shall you tell of a good yemàn,
His name was Robyn Hode.

(Traditional ballad, 'A Lytell Geste of Robyn Hode', c. 1491)

Clad in a tunic of Lincoln green, with a feather in his cap and an arrow poised with deadly precision in his longbow, Robin Hood is one of the most familiar figures in English folklore. An outlaw with a heart of gold, who robbed the rich only to give to the poor, he dwelt in the dark forest of Sherwood, plotting against the evil Sheriff of Nottingham and carousing around the campfire with his comrades or 'Merry Men', including Little John, Will Scarlet and Friar Tuck. This is the clear picture that we have of him, thanks largely to children's books and a whole panoply of dramatisations for TV and cinema. But how long has the story of Robin Hood been around? And was he a real person?

The line 'Robyn hod in scherewod stod' ('Robin Hood in Sherwood stood') occurs in a short poem dating from about 1410, preserved in Lincoln Cathedral. It is thought that the earliest ballads about his adventures may have originated in the 13th or 14th century, and were passed down verbally from one generation to the next until they were reproduced in print in the early 1500s. Some stories are set in Barnsdale Forest in South Yorkshire, but it is Sherwood (from *Sciryuda*, meaning 'shire wood') in Nottinghamshire that has retained the strongest connection.

As the haunt of swashbuckling adventurers, Sherwood has all the right attributes. Pollen samples show that there has been woodland here since the end of the last glacial period, some 11,000 years ago. After the retreat of the ice, the land was colonised by birch, willow, elm and oak; prehistoric hunter-gatherers stalking deer and boar left a scatter of flint tools in their wake. As it evolved, the forest was shaped and managed by humans who felled trees and created clearings that became patches of heathland.

By the 1300s, the terms 'robehod', 'hobbehod' and 'hobbe the robber' were used to describe any notorious robber, real or imagined.

By the 12th century, Sherwood Forest occupied some 100,000 acres (40,500 hectares) and covered almost a quarter of the county of Nottinghamshire. Today when we hear the word 'forest' we imagine a densely wooded area, but originally it described land of any kind that was reserved for the sport of medieval kings. In Kings Clipstone, a royal hunting lodge known as King John's Palace welcomed a succession of monarchs from Henry II in the late 12th century to Richard II some 200 years later. A network of foresters patrolled the woods and meted out severe punishments to poachers.

On this basis Sherwood Forest sounds an unlikely refuge for anyone trying to evade capture, but this is exactly how Robin Hood is depicted: living secretly in the depths of the forest, he is so finely tuned to his surroundings that he senses the approach of strangers and watches them unseen, while deciding whether or not to let them pass. This quality has persuaded some folklorists that he is a 'descendant' of the Green Man, an ancient symbol of rebirth who haunted the greenwood, and whose power was acknowledged every spring.

More prosaically, Robin is portrayed as an outlaw. In the 21st century (and especially in movies!) this term has an undeniable appeal: a maverick, a rough diamond, unable to conform with society's rules but still saving the day and defeating the villains by fire and sword. But in Anglo-Saxon times, an outlaw was an offender who had committed serious crimes. To be outlawed was tantamount to a sentence of death: it was said that you 'bore the wolf's head', meaning that anybody could lawfully kill you.

As for tracing a single historical figure who can be identified as the original Robin, the trail gets bogged down in a swamp of speculation. In his book *In Search of England* (1999), historian Michael Wood considers the strongest candidate to be one Robert Hood, outlawed in 1226–27, who lived in the north of England at a time when foreign clergy with English benefices were being captured, ransomed or robbed. During the desperate winter of 1231, rebel bands, some of whom wore their heads hooded, seized barns full of grain and sold it at low prices or gave it away to the poor.

By the 1300s, the terms 'robehod', 'hobbehod' and 'hobbe the robber' were used to describe any notorious robber, real or imagined. Robin Hood, if he ever existed, had vanished back into the forest and was reappearing as the legendary leader of a band of renegades whose adventures were constantly being reinvented and embellished. Their conduct was rough and ready, with the tendency to shoot first and ask questions later, but they still had a clear moral code, battling against corruption on behalf of the poor.

During the 15th and 16th centuries, the figure of Robin Hood played a central role in May Day pageants up and down the country. On May Day in 1515, King Henry VIII and his court went out to Shooter's Hill where they were met by a company of yeomen dressed as Robin and his Merry Men and invited to a feast in the greenwood. Four hundred years later, Sir Walter Scott's Robin of Locksley is a 19th-century superhero: "'This must be the devil, and no man of flesh and blood," whispered the yeomen to each other; "such archery was never seen since a bow was first bent in Britain.'" (*Ivanhoe*, 1819.) Fast-forward to the 1991 adventure film and Kevin Costner's 'Prince of Thieves' is

> *Sherwood Forest still contains Europe's largest collection of ancient oaks.*

fighting to the death with Alan Rickman's sadistic Sheriff of Nottingham.

If visitors to the modern-day Sherwood Forest don't catch a glimpse of Robin Hood running fleet-footed through the trees, they can gaze up at the Major Oak, reckoned to be between 800 and 1,100 years old, in whose shade the Merry Men are said to have gathered. Although the forest has been significantly depleted in recent centuries, it still contains Europe's largest collection of ancient oaks.

WANDLEBURY HILL

Old Gogmagog, a Hill of long and great renowne ....

(Michael Drayton, Song 21,
Poly-Olbion, Part 2, 1622)

The many walkers who climb up to the Iron Age hill fort on top of Wandlebury Hill, just south of Cambridge, are probably unaware that beneath their feet is the long-lost figure of a giant named Gogmagog. Once clearly scoured out of the white chalk, he exists now only in scraps of folk memory and in brief, but tantalising, written accounts.

The two separate names of 'Gog' and 'Magog' occur in early religious scripts and legends across Europe and the Middle East, and it is thought that they were melded together by the 12th-century writer Geoffrey of Monmouth. Using a creative mix of history, legend and imagination, he tells how the warriors Brutus and Corineus of Troy came to Britain and found it inhabited by giants. They killed them all except the fiercest, called Goëmagot (Gogmagog) who was 'in stature twelve cubits, and of such prodigious strength that at one shake he pulled up an oak as if it had been a hazel wand'. (*Historia regum Britanniae*, c. 1136.)

Corineus was keen to try his strength against Goëmagot, so Brutus arranged a wrestling match. Locked in a deadly tussle, the two gasped and strained until Corineus, with a supreme effort, hoisted Goëmagot onto his shoulders and carried him to the coast, where he threw him off a cliff and into the sea.

> *The archaeologist T.C. Lethbridge became convinced that a second, much more ancient, figure lay beneath the turf.*

The whereabouts of this contest is vague, but the story may have influenced activities which took place on Wandlebury Hill. From the late 1500s, and possibly earlier, it was the venue for a gathering, organised by students of Cambridge University, known as the Gogmagog Olympics. The hill fort made a convenient amphitheatre, and within it the enormous figure of a giant had been cut into the chalk; this may have been ancient, but some writers suggest it was the work of the students themselves.

Quite appropriately, sporting contests in the Gogmagog Olympics included wrestling, along with running, jumping and shooting. In July 1620 a student named Simonds D'Ewes was excited to hear that a prize bull had been brought along for some bull-baiting. By that time the event 'had become notorious as a place of resort', and was frowned upon by the University governors, so when D'Ewes rode up the hill with his tutor and saw all the stalls set up, he took care to emphasise that 'he had never in his life been here before'. (J.H. Marsden, *College Life in the Time of James the First, as illustrated by an unpublished diary of Sir Symonds D'Ewes*, 1851.)

Obscured by the building of a mansion house in the 18th century, this chalk giant was largely forgotten until the 1950s, when the archaeologist T.C. Lethbridge became convinced that a second, much more ancient, figure lay beneath the turf. While the giant on the hilltop could never have been seen from a distance, Lethbridge claimed that this older figure was cut into the slope below it and had been visible from the nearby village of Sawston until the early 19th century. An old story of a buried gold chariot added to the mystery.

Lethbridge tried to locate the second figure using a method he devised himself. He probed the ground at regular intervals with a steel bar and placed pegs where it sank deeper, because he believed that the scouring of a chalk figure created artificial hollows. When plotted on paper, the pegs suggested a vague but intriguing tableau of shapes and figures. Lethbridge interpreted them as a Celtic goddess whom he called Magog, a sun god whom he called Gog, a horse and chariot, and a crescent moon. Going back to the hillside, he removed the turf to reveal the corresponding chalk pattern beneath.

However, Lethbridge's excitement was short-lived: doubt was cast on the validity of his methods and his findings were attributed to natural geological formations. His chalk figures have since been reabsorbed, but aerial photographs of them survive.

Had Lethbridge discovered something truly ancient, or had he been beguiled by folklore? Afterwards, he reported seeing some medieval graffiti in a local church that exactly resembled his goddess. But later investigations found no evidence of his chalk figures.

There is another old legend attached to Wandlebury Hill. In his *Otia Imperialia* (c. 1211), Gervase of Tilbury explains that, if a warrior rides alone into the hill fort on a moonlit night and calls out 'Knight to knight, come forth!', a ghostly horserider will appear out of the darkness and accept the challenge to a duel.

This was put to the test by a Norman knight named Osbert FitzHugh. As predicted, the apparition responded to his call and the two knights rode furiously towards each other with their lances levelled. FitzHugh unseated the phantom and seized his horse, which he took away with him; it was a black stallion, wild and uncontrollable, and at dawn it broke free and disappeared. But FitzHugh was left with a permanent reminder of the contest, because the ghostly knight had thrown his lance and struck him in the leg. The wound healed, but reopened every year on the anniversary of the contest.

SUTTON HOO

It was the discovery of a lifetime. In 1939, an archaeologist named Basil Brown dug into a low grassy mound, one of several that are clustered in a field close to the River Deben in Suffolk, and found the grave of an Anglo-Saxon king. Out of the crumbling soil emerged jaw-dropping artefacts that were beyond an archaeologist's wildest dreams: an elaborate gold belt buckle of astonishing workmanship; exquisite gold shoulder clasps and sword fittings inlaid with garnets; ornate silver bowls and spoons, some originating from the Eastern Mediterranean; and pieces of a magnificent masked helmet whose facial features had been designed to form the shape of a flying dragon.

In total, 263 finds – including the fittings from a decorated shield, fragments of a maple wood lyre and silver-gilt fittings from two enormous auroch-horn drinking vessels – were recovered from the burial chamber. Many were luxury items, displaying exquisite craftsmanship. But what made the discovery even more extraordinary was the setting in which the king and all his riches had been laid to rest. A buried ship, whose wooden hull had long ago rotted away, had left behind a ghostly imprint in the soil. Its elegant, tapering shape was lined with hundreds of iron rivets.

Landowner Edith Pretty had had a long-standing curiosity about the mounds that lay a few hundred yards from her house, but it was a chance meeting with a local historian at the Woodbridge Flower Show in 1937 that inspired her to begin a proper excavation. Edith had been widowed for three years and had a young son; perhaps her interest in archaeology was a welcome distraction from her grief. Ipswich Museum recommended a local self-taught archaeologist by the name of Basil Brown. She offered him 30 shillings a week, the help of two labourers and accommodation in a nearby cottage. It was a partnership that yielded spectacular results.

During his first season at Sutton Hoo in 1938, Brown excavated three mounds – all of which had been robbed in former centuries, leaving only tantalising glimpses behind. Significantly, he found a number of iron ship rivets in what is now called Mound 2. As he turned these over in his hands, he would no doubt have been reminded of another ship burial, uncovered in the 1800s just 10 miles (16km) away at Snape; perhaps he felt a thrill of excitement as he imagined what might still lie buried in the ground beneath his feet.

The following year, Brown turned his attention to the largest mound, now called Mound 1. He was relieved to find that, although treasure-seekers had dug into it, they had missed the burial chamber by yards. It turned out to be the richest intact early medieval grave in northern Europe.

Owing to the acidity of the soil, any organic remains were poorly preserved. One of the many mysteries of Sutton Hoo was whether a body had been laid to rest in the ship, but the placement of the grave goods, along with later phosphate analysis, confirmed that this was the case. The grave's most likely occupant was Rædwald, an Anglo-Saxon king of East Anglia who died around AD 625. Rædwald was a member of the powerful Wuffinga dynasty. The foundations of a large and elaborate timber hall, thought to be a royal residence mentioned by The Venerable Bede in the 8th century, have been discovered close by, at Rendlesham.

Rædwald's life bridged a period of momentous change in the religious beliefs of the Anglo-Saxons, as pagan worship gave way to Christianity. According to The Venerable Bede, Rædwald was baptised but was drawn back to his old pagan beliefs, and he worshipped at a temple with two altars. While some of the grave goods at Sutton Hoo may suggest the influence of Christianity – for example the silver spoons and bowls – others are magnificently pagan.

For the people of Sutton Hoo, waterways were not barriers but arteries of trade, communication and ideas. Connections across the North Sea, to areas such as Scandinavia and Germany, would have been keenly felt. Norse mythology tells of a sacred ash tree named Yggdrasil which stood at the centre of nine worlds and was a meeting-place of the gods. Yggdrasil's branches extended into the heavens and a spring flowed from beneath each of its three roots. The war god Odin (known as Woden to the Anglo-Saxons) is said to have travelled to one of these springs, which was guarded by a god named Mímir. The spring contained all the wisdom and knowledge of the world, and Odin wanted to drink from it, but Mímir demanded one of his eyes in exchange for a single draught of water. Odin agreed to this sacrifice, drank from the spring and was endowed with tremendous wisdom.

> '... under that root which turns toward the Rime-Giants is Mímir's Well, wherein wisdom and understanding are stored; and he is called Mímir, who keeps the well. He is full of ancient lore, since he drinks of the well from the Gjallar-Horn. Thither came Allfather [Odin] and craved one drink of the well; but he got it not until he had laid his eye in pledge.'
>
> (*The Prose Edda*, Snorri Sturluson, 13th century, trans. A.G. Brodeur, 1916)

One of the intricate details of the Sutton Hoo helmet may be rooted in this mythology as a projection of power, the helmet's owner possibly claiming divine descent with an allusion to the one-eyed Odin. The garnet cloisonné cells lining the right eyebrow are backed with gold foil which reflects the light, but there is no foil beneath the garnets along the left eyebrow – a deliberate omission, perhaps, which would have made the left eyebrow look dull by comparison. In the shadowy interior of a feasting hall, where the flames of a blazing fire would have made a warrior's jewels flash and gleam, the wearer of this magnificent helmet may well have appeared one-eyed, like Odin himself.

The garnet-eyed dragon that spreads its wings across the helmet's mask calls to mind a powerful scene from the Old English epic poem *Beowulf*, which is set in 6th-century Scandinavia. A fire-breathing dragon guards a burial mound and wreaks dreadful revenge when its treasure is stolen, burning Beowulf's throne hall to the ground. Beowulf prepares to confront it, knowing that he is about to meet his end; before he dies, he leaves instructions about his burial: 'Bid the famous warriors build a shining mound after the funeral fire, upon a headland by the sea. It shall tower high upon Whale's Ness as a memorial to my people; so that the seafarers in after days shall name it the mound of Beowulf, as they urge their steep ships from afar over the misty deep.' (*Beowulf*, lines 2802–8, trans. Hilda R. Ellis Davidson, from 'The Hill of the Dragon – Anglo-Saxon Burial Mounds in Literature and Archaeology', *Folklore* journal, 1950.)

The image of a burial mound as a landmark is suddenly a vivid one, in this case bearing witness to the courage and power of a great war-leader. Meanwhile, as we gaze in awe at the treasures of Sutton Hoo, perhaps the most fascinating elements are the things that we cannot see: our attention is riveted by the empty eye-holes of the helmet, and we look through them into a dark and mysterious past that is peopled by warrior-heroes, monsters and vengeful gods.

THE GREAT STONE OF LYNG

AD 870: This year the army rode across Mercia into
East-Anglia, and took up their winter quarters at
Thetford: and the same winter king Edmund fought
against them, and the Danes got the victory, and slew
the king ....

(*Anglo-Saxon Chronicle*, 9th century,
trans. J.A. Giles, 1914)

Sometime towards the end of the last glacial period, about 11,000
years ago, a retreating ice sheet dumped a huge boulder in the
landscape of what is now Norfolk. This in itself was nothing
unusual – these boulders, termed 'erratics', are scattered across
Britain, testifying to the immense power of glaciers as they
plucked and transported rocks far from their place of origin, later
dropping them randomly as the climate slowly warmed. What
makes the Great Stone of Lyng so peculiar are the human stories
that have grown up around it.

An irregular, roughly rounded lump measuring about 6 feet
(2 metres) in length and covered in cushions of green moss, the
stone looks innocent enough. It lies amid some woodland on the
edge of a 'hollow way', a track created by the footfall of centuries.
But folklore paints it in a darker light. An old superstition warns
that it will bleed when pricked with a pin because blood was shed
close by, either in battle or in sacrifice.

Local people would speak of an eerie quietness in the
surrounding woodland; birds were said to be silent there, and

wayfarers on the path glimpsed the ghosts of warriors and nuns in the twilight. In the 1800s the stone was so notorious that local children were allowed out of school early on winter evenings, so that they could pass it before it got dark.

A local landowner, so it is said, believed that there was treasure buried beneath the stone and harnessed his team of horses to try and move it, hoping to dig there. Needless to say, it refused to budge. All these stories could be dismissed as fanciful; on the other hand, they might preserve some tantalising fragments of historical events, and in particular the proximity of a fierce battle and a community of nuns.

> *Local people would speak of an eerie quietness in the surrounding woodland; birds were said to be silent there, and wayfarers on the path glimpsed the ghosts of warriors and nuns in the twilight.*

The tale begins with the death of Edmund, a king of East Anglia, in AD 869*. At that time, raiding parties of Vikings were making devastating attacks on coastal communities in eastern England and encroaching ever further inland. Edmund may have been killed in a skirmish, but another account tells how the Vikings, led by Ivar the Boneless, captured him and demanded that he renounce Christianity and act as their puppet king. He

---

* The *Anglo-Saxon Chronicle* gives a date of AD 870, but some years in this document begin in September.

refused, so they tied him to a tree and shot at him with arrows. Then they beheaded him, threw his head into a bramble thicket and went on their way.

Miraculously, Edmund's followers managed to relocate his head because (according to one story) it called out to them from the bushes; another story tells how it was being guarded by a wolf. Either way, the head was reunited with the body and buried, so one tradition says, close to the Great Stone of Lyng which served as a convenient marker. Later, a chapel and nunnery were established near the spot, so that prayers could be offered for Edmund's soul.

Pilgrims to St Edmund's Chapel reported many miracles of healing, a phenomenon which suggests the presence of saintly relics.

How much of this is history and how much is folklore? We know that in AD 903, the body of Edmund was moved to a Benedictine monastery in Beodericsworth, which would later become Bury St Edmunds. But by this time he was venerated as a saint and stories of the events leading up to his death were probably embellished to accentuate his holiness. The exact location of the battle, and his subsequent death and burial, are still matters for debate. The place where he died was named as *Haeglisdun* by the chronicler Abbo of Fleury, writing around AD 985, and one claimant for the location is Hoxne in Suffolk. Another possibility is Hellesdon, a few miles south-east of Lyng. If Edmund died at Hellesdon, his body could have been carried up the River

Wensum and buried near the Great Stone of Lyng, which was no doubt a well-known landmark. What gives this theory more credibility is that the stone is named on old maps as St Edmund's Stone, and the surrounding wood was called King's Grove.

What's more, there is tangible evidence of a chapel here, dedicated to Saint Edmund: quietly crumbling in a nearby field, a remnant of an archway is all that survives (the very earliest chapel was likely built of wood). Pilgrims to St Edmund's Chapel reported many miracles of healing, a phenomenon which suggests the presence of saintly relics, which were traditionally protected by a community of nuns. In 1437, permission was granted to the prioress of Thetford for an annual fair to be held at Lyng on the date of Edmund's death, which was 20 November, and this tradition was upheld until the 18th century.

It is said that, when the chapel was finally abandoned, its bells were cast into the river, and that they can sometimes still be heard ringing. There is also a story about a silver chalice, found by two boatmen on a stretch of river near the chapel; as they quarrelled over it, the chalice slipped out of their grasp and fell back into the water.

Ironically, Edmund was later revered by the Danes who settled in England, and he is considered to be England's first patron saint. In 1020 King Cnut (a king of both England and Denmark) founded an abbey around Edmund's shrine in Bury St Edmunds.

HETHEL OLD THORN

With the passing of centuries, many trees have become familiar and much-loved landmarks in the British countryside. Veterans of mind-boggling age, they might be towering and majestic, or gaunt and gnarled; they might even be broken remnants, still clinging on to life and resolutely putting out leaves and flowers and fruits as the seasons turn. They have seen generations come and go, and have heard the footfall of labourers and travellers on the old tracks, as well as the tramp of invading armies. They are silent but living witnesses to the unfolding of history.

In a field close to All Saints Church at Hethel in Norfolk is one of these remarkable trees. It is a hawthorn (*Crataegus monogyna*) and it is possibly the largest of its kind in England; with an age of at least 700 years, it is certainly one of our oldest hawthorns. It stands within the Norfolk Wildlife Trust's smallest nature reserve, set up for its own protection and occupying an area of just 0.062 acres (0.025 hectares).

In the mid-18th century the naturalist Robert Marsham measured the girth of the trunk at more than 20 feet (6 metres); a hundred years later, it had shrunk to 14 feet (4 metres), possibly as a result of portions splitting away from the main trunk, but its branches still covered an area 31 yards (28 metres) in circumference. It was described as being encrusted with lichen, and every winter local people braved its thorns to reach the mistletoe which festooned its crown.

Writing in 1841, local landowner Hudson Gurney described the tree's curious appearance: 'Not only the bark of the hollow tree is as hard and as heavy as iron, but every branch, most curiously inter-involved, is a hollow tube into which you may put your arm, all the interior wood being gone.' (James Grigor, *The Eastern Arboretum, or Register of Remarkable Trees, Seats, Gardens, &c. in the County of Norfolk*, 1841.)

According to local tradition, the Hethel Old Thorn was the meeting-place for an insurrection of peasant farmers in the reign of King John. In medieval times, meetings were often held under boundary trees, and it is likely that this was its original purpose. In his book *The History of the Countryside* (1986), Oliver Rackham explains that thorn trees are by far the commonest tree species mentioned in Anglo-Saxon charters, which were drawn up to define the boundaries of land ownership.

Hawthorn trees are associated with witchcraft; in fact, another name for the Hethel Old Thorn is the Witch of Hethel.

An article in *The Gentleman's Magazine* (7 November 1856) wonders if the tree is 'still living witness ... of Roman conquest, Dutch forays, and Druidical superstition'. This might be stretching possibility too far ... but there is also a legend that it sprouted from the staff of Joseph of Arimathea when he brought the young Jesus Christ with him to England. A similar story was woven around the Holy Thorn of Glastonbury, inspiring William Blake to compose his famous poem 'Jerusalem'.

Hawthorn has been used for hedging since Saxon times; the

word 'hawthorn' comes from the Anglo-Saxon *hagedorn*, meaning 'hedge-thorn'. 'Hag', meaning 'witch', shares the same root, and hawthorn trees are associated with witchcraft; in fact, another name for the Hethel Old Thorn is the Witch of Hethel. Fairies are said to dwell in the branches of hawthorn trees and there are many tales of people being spirited away to the underworld if they

lingered too long in their shade. Hawthorn leaves adorn the faces of Green Men, ancient symbols of rebirth that can be found carved in medieval churches.

Hawthorns were often spared the woodcutter's axe because it was believed that cutting them down would invite calamity. Thanks to the persistence of this superstition, ancient examples like the Hethel Old Thorn still survive. But a sprig of hawthorn had powerful properties; in the 14th century, Sir John Mandeville wrote: 'For he that beareth a branch on hym thereof, no thundre, ne no maner of tempest, may dere hym, ne in the howse that it is ynne may non evil ghost enter.' (H.N. Ellacombe, *The Plant-lore and Garden-craft of Shakespeare*, 1896.)

As the Hethel Old Thorn became more aged and sprawling its branches required the support of props. Every May Day, local children would dance around the village maypole and then run to the thorn tree in a race to be the first to count its props. No doubt its abundant foamy blossom was gathered for May Day garlands, celebrating the freshness and fertility of the Earth in springtime.

The Witch of Hethel still has a powerful presence. Gertrude Clarke Nuttall hit on a deep truth when she wrote about the hawthorn: 'There is no tree that is more deeply enshrined in the traditions of our country and in the affections of Englishmen.' (*Trees and How They Grow,* 1913.)

NORTHERN ENGLAND

ALDERLEY EDGE

Early one summer morning, so the story goes, a farmer from Mobberley in Cheshire was riding his white mare across Alderley Edge. He was on his way to Macclesfield horse fair, where he hoped to sell his beautiful mount for a good sum of money. Suddenly, a tall man clad in a long flowing cloak stepped out in front of him and commanded him to stop.

'I know the purpose of your journey,' he told the farmer, 'and I will buy your horse myself, to save you the trouble.' The farmer was suspicious; impatiently, he dismissed the stranger and urged the mare on. The man called after him: 'Go, then, if you must! But you will find no other buyer for that horse. And when you return empty-handed, I shall be here, waiting!' The farmer laughed scornfully, but to his astonishment he found that the stranger's prophecy came true. While the mare was greatly admired, no one offered to buy her. Dispirited, he was riding her home that evening when he saw the stranger waiting for him by the track, leaning on his wooden staff. As he drew closer he was wondering what to say, but the stranger spoke first. 'Follow me,' he said.

Intrigued, the farmer followed the man along an unfamiliar path until they came to a massive rock. The man advised the farmer to dismount and then touched the rock with his staff; instantly it split in two, revealing iron gates across the entrance to a dark tunnel. Startled, the mare reared up. Struggling to control her, the farmer demanded to know what was going on. 'Don't be afraid,' replied the man as he opened the gates. 'You shall soon behold a sight that no mortal eye has ever seen.'

Leading his horse, the bemused farmer was guided down the tunnel and into a candlelit cave. There, all over the stony floor, men in silver armour lay asleep beside their pure white horses; close by, a heap of treasure gleamed with gold and jewels. But the farmer's gaze was riveted on the stranger, because he knew now that he was Merlin, the legendary wizard. 'One horse is missing,' explained Merlin, 'and your white mare makes the company complete. Take whatever you wish in payment, and go in peace. But remember that, when England is in peril, King Arthur and his knights will wake and ride out valiantly across the plain.'

The farmer did as he was bidden and returned to the daylight. Try as he might, he could never relocate the entrance to the cave.

> And since his death full many a man
> Has sought that iron gate;
> And wander'd near that grey hill-side
> At early morn and late:
> But still the gate is kept from view,
> By Merlin watch'd each hour;
> And will be till King Arthur rides,
> With all his knightly power ...

(J. Roscoe, 'The Iron Gate – A Legend of Alderley',
Blackwood's Magazine, 1839)

Just how old is the legend of Alderley Edge? Perhaps we will never know. In the earliest versions, the wizard and the knights are not named, and the Arthurian connection comes later. This sandstone escarpment in the Cheshire plain has been a significant place for millennia. Bronze Age people came here to mine copper around

1900 BC, and shallow shafts from this period can still be seen. The Romans mined here too: a mineshaft dating from the 1st century AD was found to conceal a hoard of later (4th-century) Roman coins.

Mining continued until the 1800s, but nowadays visitors come to Alderley Edge to admire the stunning views and examine the curious man-made features that perpetuate its legends. Hidden in the woods, a 'Druid's Circle' of recumbent stones is actually a 19th-century folly. At the Wizard's Well, where water from a natural spring flows into a stone trough, an enigmatic face is carved into the rock. An inscription beneath reads: 'Drink of this and take thy fill, for the water falls by the Wizhard's will.' The face is believed to have been carved in the 19th century by local stonemason Robert Garner – an ancestor of the author Alan Garner, whose children's books were inspired by the legends of Alderley Edge.

> An echoing sigh, like waves slowly rippling on a summer shore, rose and fell upon the air; and before the children's eyes were the sleeping knights in their silver armour, each beside his milk-white mare, just as Gowther had described them in the legend, their gentle breathing filling the cave with its sweet sound. And all around and over the motionless figures the cold, white flames played silently.

(Alan Garner, *The Weirdstone of Brisingamen*, 1960)

Geologically, Alderley Edge is one of the best-known locations in Britain for Triassic-age sandstone; the rocks were laid down from about 250 million years ago, in successive layers deposited by wind and water. Minerals associated with copper, such as malachite, azurite and chrysocolla, sparkle on the walls of old mineshafts in brilliant hues of blue, turquoise and green. It's tempting to imagine that these are the remnants of the treasure that Merlin offered so generously in exchange for King Arthur's last horse.

MOTHER SHIPTON'S CAVE

As the River Nidd flows through its gorge at Knaresborough in North Yorkshire, it passes beneath a number of curious caves. One of these is reputed to be the birthplace of a prophetess named Ursula Southeil, better known as Mother Shipton.

Every part of Ursula's story is based on folklore: in *The Lore of the Land* (2005), Jennifer Westwood and Jacqueline Simpson observe that her name doesn't appear in parish records, so even her existence cannot be verified. But the stories are surprisingly specific in their detail. She is said to have been born around 1488 to a 15-year-old girl from Knaresborough called Agatha Southeil, who had fled to the cave to escape persecution because she had become pregnant outside wedlock. Ursula's father was unknown and her mother was soon admitted into a convent, leaving her in the care of a foster-mother.

Over the centuries, storytellers have let their imaginations run riot about Ursula's appearance. They claimed that, as a young woman, she resembled the stereotypical witch, with a crooked nose, piercing eyes and a pointed hat. Shunned by most local people, she lived a simple life in her cave and ventured alone into the forest, gathering wild plants to make herbal remedies. In 1512 she married Tobias Shipton, a carpenter from York, who died shortly after their marriage.

Fear of the unknown probably inspired the first rumours about Ursula. People whispered that she was the child of the Devil and a nun, and rode in a chariot drawn by stags and attended by imps. But more to the point, she could foretell future events. One of the most popular tales involved Cardinal Wolsey, the Archbishop of York and Lord Chancellor to King Henry VIII. On hearing that Wolsey intended to visit York, Ursula predicted that he would see the city, but would never enter it. She was proved right: during his travels, Wolsey halted within sight of

People whispered that she was the child of the Devil and a nun, and rode in a chariot drawn by stags and attended by imps.

York, but was arrested before entering its walls. He died of natural causes on his way back to London to answer charges of treason.

As the fame of Ursula's prophetic wisdom continued to spread, she became known as Mother Shipton, even though she had no children. She is said to have foretold the marriage and death of Anne Boleyn, and the execution of Mary, Queen of Scots. In his diary on 20 October 1666, Samuel Pepys wrote that, on receiving the first news of the Great Fire of London, Prince Rupert of the Rhine commented that 'now Shipton's prophecy is out' – in other words, now he understood what she meant. Exactly what he was referring to, however, is something of a mystery, as not all of

Mother Shipton's sayings were recorded in writing – and, unfortunately, many were fabricated by later authors with the benefit of hindsight.

One of these authors was Charles Hindley, who, in 1862, produced a pamphlet entitled 'The Life, Prophecies and Death of the Famous Mother Shipton'. With more than a dash of creativity, Hindley included events and innovations from the Victorian era which Mother Shipton had 'foreseen' – among them steam power, railways and the Crimean War. Later, he admitted that he had added these details himself.

It is now impossible to tell which of Mother Shipton's predictions are genuinely hers. Hindley's paper includes a claim that 'Under water men shall walk / Shall ride, shall sleep shall talk', which could refer to submarines. Another, stating that 'The world to an end shall come / In eighteen hundred and eighty-one' caused mass panic at the beginning of that year and it was only with the passing of time that Mother Shipton was found to have been mistaken. But there is an element of truth in the line 'Around the world thoughts shall fly / In the twinkling of an eye', especially if it is applied to the invention of the internet.

The cave in which Mother Shipton reputedly lived is a natural geological feature. It is formed from tufa, a type of limestone that is deposited by running water. Underground springs containing dissolved minerals emerge from the sides of the gorge and spill down into the River Nidd, leaving behind layers of tufa that build up on the cliff faces. At the Dropping Well, close to Mother Shipton's Cave, an entire rock face has been smoothed and sculpted in this way, and beneath its projecting rim hang rows of objects (shoes, toys, hats, gloves) that visitors have left to petrify in the constantly dripping water – a process that takes anything from three to six months. No doubt Mother Shipton's reputation was enhanced by her apparent ability to turn household objects into stone!

BRIMHAM ROCKS

Dark mountain desert, awful piles of stone –
Like giant ruins! how ye seem to mock
The puny efforts of such feeble things
As we, frail mortals, are! Far round I see
Strange broken columns rise – shapelessly grand;
 As if some more than merely human race
Had made their dwellings here.

(Rev. James Holme, 'Brimham Rocks' from *Leisure Musings and Devotional Meditations*, c. 1835)

In the 18th century, visitors to Brimham Rocks (also known as Brimham Crags) found themselves groping for words to describe the monstrous structures that confronted them. Among them was the Welsh writer and naturalist Thomas Pennant, who climbed up to this windswept moorland site during a visit to Yorkshire in 1777. As he gazed around at the alien-looking landscape of gargantuan rocks, each one smoothed and sculpted into preposterous shapes, he listened to his companion, Moses

Griffith, who was quite emphatic about their origins. This, he explained to Pennant, was the handiwork of druids.

But Pennant, while listening politely, had private doubts. He wrote: 'My fancy could not create remains of the works of art, or relics of Druidical superstition.' (*Tour from Alston-Moor to Harrowgate and Brimham Crags*, 1804.) Instead, he believed he was witnessing a landscape that was exposed following the Great Flood, as described in the Bible; he theorised that the rocks had been submerged in mud which had since been washed away by lesser deluges.

At the time, neither Pennant nor Griffith could have guessed the real geological processes that resulted in the extraordinary formations at Brimham Rocks. It was, after all, many decades before 19th-century scientists such as Louis Agassiz and James Geikie began to look at Britain's landscape and see the impact of long-lost ice-sheets and the scouring of glaciers. And even with the benefit of 21st-century science, the timescales involved are hard to comprehend.

First, the rocks themselves had to be formed. About 400 million years ago, two of the Earth's tectonic plates (the North America and Eurasia plates) collided, and threw up a vast mountain range in what would become northern Britain. Many millions of years later – a blink of an eye in geological time – fast-flowing rivers poured out of these mountains, depositing deep layers of silt, sand and pebbles, which were slowly compressed into a type of sandstone called millstone grit.

Fast forward to the (relatively) recent past – specifically, the last glacial period, between about 30,000 and 18,000 years ago, when a glacier gouged out the Nidderdale Valley. Brimham's millstone grit resisted erosion by the glacier itself, but when it was exposed above the ice it was blasted by a savage wind carrying fine particles of sand. This wind scoured the rock surfaces smooth while forcing its way into cracks and lines of weakness, wearing away softer layers to create a panorama of mind-boggling shapes.

Now lying at nearly 1,000 feet (305 metres) above sea level, at first glance Brimham Rocks resemble the ruins of some ancient civilisation that has left behind enormous temples and statues of its gods. Bastions of rock rise in bulging 'storeys' many metres high, tunnels pierce them at ground level, and gigantic columns perch on minuscule pedestals, looking ready to topple at the slightest touch. Formations have been named according to their shape by generations of tourists: the Serpent's Head, the Frog and Tortoise, the Dancing Bear, the Cannon Rocks and the Lovers' Leap. The last feature is the spot from which two lovers are said to have leaped in despair, having been banned from marrying by a disapproving parent – but they survived and, because this was seen as divine intervention, they were allowed to marry.

Early visitors to Brimham Rocks noticed that some of the precariously balanced boulders would rock back and forth with only the lightest pressure. These 'logan stones' or 'rocking stones' were associated with the druids, who, according to Thomas Pennant, 'impressed on their votaries that the moving of them was miraculous, and a power reserved to their sacred orders'. (*Tour from Alston-Moor to Harrowgate and Brimham Crags*, 1804.)

In the late 1700s the antiquary Hayman Rooke suggested that the druids had used the site as a temple, and that they might have perforated some of the rocks for the purpose of delivering oracles. He also noted that a feature called the Noon Stone was said to cast a shadow indicating the time of day, and that since ancient times a fire had been kindled there every Midsummer's Eve.

In the writings of Rooke and Pennant, the term 'druid' was intended to conjure a robed and bearded figure, something between a sorcerer and a prophet, belonging to that mysterious fraternity of people described by the Romans. Until the 19th century very little was known about the prehistory of Britain, and to many writers druids were its oldest conceivable inhabitants.

We cannot know for sure whether druids actually frequented Brimham Rocks; there is no evidence of their presence, nor is there any trace of Iron Age settlement. Close by, rock carvings and a prehistoric cemetery hint at

At first glance Brimham Rocks resemble the ruins of some ancient civilisation that has left behind enormous temples and statues of its gods.

some ancient significance, blurred now by the vivid imaginings of 18th- and 19th-century tourists. But snatches of folklore survive: according to the Yorkshire writer Edmund Bogg, who spoke to local residents in 1895, it was long held to be the abode of spirits, and this superstition was still current. He was told that it had a natural echo, which was a spirit's voice; they called it 'the Son of the Rocks'.

KING ARTHUR'S ROUND TABLE AND MAYBURGH HENGE

Ah Minstrels! when the Table Round
Arose, with all its warriors crown'd
There was a theme for bards to sound
In triumph to their string!

(Sir Walter Scott, *The Bridal of Triermain*, 1813)

According to legend, King Arthur desired a round table to be made for himself and his knights so that they could all be seated as equals. But how big was it? The number of knights varies enormously from one story to the next – sometimes it is 12, and sometimes hundreds! – and there was always a place left unoccupied, called the Siege Perilous or 'dangerous seat', reserved for the knight who would one day locate the Holy Grail.

Several places in Britain claim to be King Arthur's Round Table, among them a henge monument just a mile or so to the south of Penrith in Cumbria. It consists of a flat, circular platform of earth about 160 feet (50 metres) wide, surrounded by a ditch and bank. Originally it had two entrances resembling short causeways, the more northerly of which succumbed to 19th-century development; one was flanked by two standing stones, now lost.

John Leland, a 16th-century antiquary, was one of the first

visitors to record the site's Arthurian connection. He wrote: 'The Ruine is of sum caullid the Round Table and of summe Arture's Castel.' (*Itinerary of John Leland*, ed. L.T. Smith, 1910.) Thomas Pennant suggested that the henges hosted Norse duelling contests known as *hólmganga*, and in 1774 his contemporary, William Hutchinson, gave the theory an Arthurian flavour: 'We were induced to believe this was an ancient tilting ground, where in days of chivalry tournaments had been held; the approaches would answer for the career, and the circle seems sufficient to allow the champions to show their dexterity in justing and horsemanship, the whole circus being capable of receiving one thousand spectators without the ditch.' (*An Excursion to the Lakes in Westmoreland and Cumberland*, 1774.)

There was always a place left unoccupied, called the Siege Perilous or 'dangerous seat', reserved for the knight who would one day locate the Holy Grail.

Pennant and Hutchinson paint a compelling picture, but unfortunately it's impossible to correlate this with archaeological evidence. The era of King Arthur, a legendary warrior who is said to have led the Britons against Anglo-Saxon invaders, is generally placed in the 5th or early 6th century AD. This site, however, has been dated to between 2000 and 1000 BC. What's more, there is a second henge, of a similar period, just 440 yards (400 metres) away, called Mayburgh Henge.

Mayburgh Henge is considerably bigger than the Round Table,

being about 325 feet (100 metres) in diameter. A bank composed of pebbles from the River Lowther, now topped with grass and a few trees, encloses a roughly circular area with a single standing stone in the centre. Seven more stones once stood here, but most had been lost by the mid-18th century. William Stukeley, visiting in about 1723, saw a number of them, but by the time Thomas Pennant arrived in 1769 only one stone remained. Some stories claim that they were broken up and used for repairs to Penrith Castle in the reign of King Henry VI, or for rebuilding nearby Eamont Bridge, but these cannot be verified.

Visitors are often struck by the quietness of its interior, despite its proximity to busy roads.

There was even a third henge – now almost vanished – known as the Little Round Table. The concept of three henges close together brings to mind the Thornborough Henges in Yorkshire: was the number three significant? Historians can only speculate about their use, although it is thought that they may have hosted some kind of social or ritual activity; Mayburgh Henge in particular has the look and feel of an amphitheatre, and visitors are often struck by the quietness of its interior, despite its proximity to busy roads.

The traveller and writer Celia Fiennes rode through Penrith in 1698, during one of her cross-country explorations on horseback. She described King Arthur's Round Table as being 'a Round green spott of a Large Circumfference which they keep Cut round with a banke round it like a Bench', and she added another strand of folklore, perhaps shared by a local resident: '... its story is that it was the table a great Giant 6 yards tall used to Dine at, and there Entertain'd another of nine yards tall which he afterwards killed.' (*Through England on a Side Saddle in the Time of William and Mary, Being the Diary of Celia Fiennes,* 1888.)

Where some visitors saw giants or spurred and helmeted knights, a local innkeeper in the early 1800s saw an opportunity for a tea garden. Keen to create a flat surface for tables and chairs, he got to work levelling the bank and deepening the ditch. At the time his scheme was not considered out of the ordinary, but it does explain why pieces of broken china turn up regularly in excavations.

Meanwhile the legend endures. In Sir Walter Scott's *The Bridal of Triermain*, Sir Roland de Vaux dreams that he has seen a beautiful maiden in his chamber. Desperate to identify her, he sends his page, Henry, galloping off to consult a druid:

> He pass'd red Penrith's Table Round
> For feats of chivalry renown'd;
> Left Mayborough's mound and stones of power
> By Druids raised in magic hour,
> And traced the Eamont's winding way
> Till Ulfo's lake* beneath him lay.

* Ullswater

WINDERMERE AND CLAIFE HEIGHTS

Shut out, as it were, from the world, and enshrined in delicious seclusion, here might the weary heart dream itself away, and find the freshness of the spring-time of the spirit return upon it.

(Letitia Elizabeth Landon,
'Storrs Hall, Windermere', from
Fisher's Drawing Room Scrap Book, 1831)

It is said that Vinand, a Norse warrior, gave his name to Windermere in the 10th century, resulting in the old name of 'Winandermere' or 'Vinand's lake'. In his *Guide to the Lakes*, first published in 1810, William Wordsworth describes 'the long lake of Winandermere, stretched nearly to the sea'. Geographically speaking, meres are usually shallow bodies of water, but Windermere's bed drops away dramatically to depths of nearly 220 feet (67 metres), having been scoured out by the repeated action of glaciers.

This is England's largest lake, a slim finger of sparkling water extending for nearly 11 miles (17km) and mirroring its flanking hills and woods through every changing season. Some of Cumbria's highest fells cluster around its northern tip while, draining away from the south, the River Leven snakes its way towards the mudflats of Morecambe Bay.

Windermere rarely freezes, but during the Great Frost of 1895 it froze from end to end, and the schoolboy Arthur Ransome joined thousands of skaters gliding and turning on its steely surface. He watched ice-yachts, with masted sails and sledge-runners, racing each other up and down the lake; bonfires were lit at dusk, and the skaters, reluctant to give up their fun, carried lanterns as they shot about like fireflies. Ransome grew up to become a popular children's author, and his *Swallows and Amazons* adventures were largely inspired by the Lake District.

In Ransome's time the railways made it easy for visitors to reach Windermere from as far afield as London, but until the mid-1800s travel in the Lakes was a very different experience, necessitating arduous treks and ferry-crossings wherever they were available. About halfway down the length of Windermere, a small boat plied between a promontory called Ferry Nab on the eastern shore and the Ferry House on the opposite bank, where there was a tavern. Here the shore rises up to some wooded hills called Claife Heights.

A story tells how, one wild and stormy night in the 16th century, a call for the ferry was heard from the Nab and the boatman dutifully set out across the water. A party of travellers had been making merry in the tavern and after a while they went out to see who he was bringing back with him. But the ferryman returned alone, ashen-faced and dazed with horror. Next morning he was ill with a fever and within a short while he had died, unable to reveal what he had seen.

For weeks afterwards, eerie shrieks and howls could be heard coming from the direction of the Nab; fearing a ghostly presence, no one would row across there after dark. The local people appealed to a monk who lived on an island in the lake and on Christmas Day he exorcised the spirit, confining it to a quarry in the woods on the western shore. The spirit and the quarry both became known as 'The Crier of Claife', and as a result this is said to be the only ghost to appear on an Ordnance Survey map.

The malevolent ghost was supposedly laid to rest, but in the 19th century the quarry still had a sinister reputation. Writing in *A Complete Guide to the English Lakes* (1855), Harriet Martineau explained: 'It is still told how the foxhounds in eager chase would come to a full stop at that place; and how, within the existing generation, a schoolmaster from Colthouse, who left home to pass the Crier, was never seen more.'

It is likely that this legend was known to Beatrix Potter, walking around the woods of Claife from her nearby home in Near Sawrey. Potter purchased Hill Top in 1905, partly using the proceeds from her first children's book, *The Tale of Peter Rabbit*; she had fond memories of childhood holidays in the Lake District, having spent the summer of 1882 at Wray Castle on the shore of Windermere, and many more around the Lakes, including Derwent Water. At Hill Top, Potter found rich inspiration for more stories, including *The Tale of Tom Kitten* (1907) and its sequel, *The Tale of Samuel Whiskers* (1908).

Beatrix Potter fell in love with the Lakes. She purchased a number of hill farms in order to avoid their loss and preserve traditional ways of life, and in doing so developed a particularly keen interest in Herdwick sheep. At Wray Castle she had met Canon Hardwicke Rawnsley, a local vicar who was a passionate advocate for the protection and preservation of the Lake District's landscape. Potter shared his vision of an unspoiled countryside that could be enjoyed by everyone and she purchased more land to save it from development. In 1883, Rawnsley set up the Lake District Defence Society, and in 1895, along with Robert Hunter and Octavia Hill, he was a co-founder of the National Trust.

BLENCATHRA

Silhouetted against the skyline in the Northern Fells of the Lake District, Blencathra is a familiar and well-loved sight among climbers and local residents alike. With its multiple peaks and spurs, the highest of which (Hallsfell) rises to 2,848 feet (868 metres), it has been described as more of a small range than a single mountain.

Together with its taller neighbour, Skiddaw, Blencathra is composed of the oldest rocks in the Lake District, originating some 500 million years ago as black muds and sands that settled on an ancient seabed. From its summit, hillwalkers are rewarded with jaw-dropping views that extend as far as the Southern Uplands and Galloway Hills in Scotland, the Cheviots in Northumberland, and – on a very clear day – the Isle of Man and the Mourne Mountains of Northern Ireland.

To the Victorians, Blencathra was known by another name – 'Saddleback' – because of its saddle-shaped profile when viewed from the east. It was the fellwalker and writer Alfred Wainwright who popularised the mountain's older name of Blencathra, which is said to derive from the old Cumbric words *blain* or *blaen*, meaning 'top', and *cadeir,* meaning 'seat'. Another explanation suggests that Blencathra contains the old word *carthwr*, meaning 'working horse', again referring to its profile.

There is a third possibility, however, because local folklore asserts that Blencathra means 'Arthur's Seat'. Supporters of this last theory point to its 16th-century name, 'The Rackes of Blenkarthure' ('racke' coming from the Old Norse *reik*, a path). Like many other places throughout Britain, it is said that King Arthur and his knights sleep beneath Blencathra, ready to wake when they hear the call-to-arms at the hour of their country's need. Adding colour to this picture is the legend that, after his last battle, Arthur's sword, Excalibur, was cast into the lake of Bassenthwaite, some 12 miles (19km) away.

Sitting just to the north of Blencathra, the small glacial lake of Bowscale Tarn is said to contain a unique phenomenon: two immortal fish, which will occasionally speak to visitors. In William Wordsworth's poem 'Song at the Feast of Brougham Castle', a minstrel sings of the Good Lord Clifford, who had been given to a shepherd's family as a baby and reared as a peasant's son, but whose nobility was recognised by wild creatures:

> And both the undying fish that swim
> Through Bowscale-tarn did wait on him;
> The pair were servants of his eye
> In their immortality.

(*The Poems of William Wordsworth*, 1858)

Meanwhile it was said of Scales Tarn, nestling at the back of the mountain, that its water was so deeply shaded that the sun's rays never touched it and that the reflection of the stars could be seen on its surface at midday.

One of Blencathra's routes of ascent includes a knife-edge ridge or arête, appropriately named Sharp Edge. Described by Wainwright as being sharp enough for shaving, this 656-foot (200-metre) section can be both terrifying and exhilarating, with its rocky slopes dropping away precipitously on both sides. It is particularly dangerous in wet or foggy conditions and best reserved for very experienced fellwalkers.

In William Hutchinson's *History of the County of Cumberland* (1794) an anonymous climber describes a nerve-racking ascent of Blencathra in 1793: 'On the right, the descent to the lake looked truly awful, whilst the steep rocks on the other side were lofty, and not to be climbed by human steps ... We walked back by the side next to the lake, but to look down from thence was so terrible, I could not endure it for a moment.'

> *He had the distinct impression of being followed by invisible horsemen.*

On Midsummer's Eve in 1735, however, it was another ridge that arrested the gaze of a local farm worker. On Souter Fell (now Souther Fell), which extends north-east from Blencathra, he was astonished to see an army of men who appeared to emerge from the north end and march across the top. Although the sight lasted for over an hour, no one else witnessed it and the workman was ridiculed when he shared the story.

But two years later, also on Midsummer's Eve, the man's employer, William Lancaster, witnessed a similar spectacle: between eight and nine o'clock that evening, while riding over the fells, he had the distinct impression of being followed by invisible horsemen, and then, on turning his head, he saw a vast army, five ranks deep, proceeding along the ridge. As Lancaster and his companions watched in amazement, one or two of the mounted soldiers were seen to draw back and observe the passing troops as if taking stock of the procession, before galloping back to their stations.

This phenomenon was seen for a third time on Midsummer's Eve in 1745. On this occasion 26 local people were summoned to watch a line of men that stretched along the ridge for nearly half a mile and continued at a swift march for more than an hour. The sight was so convincing that some witnesses climbed up the ridge in the expectation of finding physical evidence, but there was not so much as a footprint to testify to the passing of an army.

Sceptics suggested that the viewers had been fooled by clouds, or a meteor, or the Northern Lights, but no one could explain why the same phenomenon had been seen on three occasions and by so many. William Lancaster later admitted that 'he never concluded they were real beings, because of the impracticability of a march over the precipices, where they seemed to come on'. (William Hutchinson, *The History of the County of Cumberland*, 1794.) However, he was adamant that it was a clear, calm evening, and a written declaration was signed by all who had seen it. The puzzle of Souther Fell's spectral army remains unsolved.

DUNMAIL RAISE

A stretch of dual carriageway on the A591 in Cumbria, which runs roughly north-south between the lakes of Grasmere and Thirlmere, splits apart to accommodate an elongated strip of ground. This 'island', isolated in the busy flow of traffic, is covered with rough grass and bracken with a handful of trees, and in the centre of it is a mound of stones. Here, according to legend, lies the last king of Cumberland. His name was Dyfnwal, and he has given his name – or another version of it – to both the cairn itself and to the pass in which it lies: Dunmail Raise.

It was here in AD 945, so the story goes, that King Dyfnwal and his Cumbrian warriors made a heroic last stand against the Anglo-Saxons, led by King Edmund I of England. Dyfnwal was mortally wounded and with his dying breath he issued an urgent order to his followers: 'My crown – bear it away; never let the Saxon flaunt it!' Escaping up into the hills, they threw it into the deep blue waters of Grisedale Tarn, where it lies to this day.

Dyfnwal was buried where he fell and a cairn of stones was raised over his grave. His two sons survived the battle but were captured and blinded by their enemies so that they would be unable to succeed their father. Every year thereafter, on the anniversary of the battle, the phantoms of the fallen warriors are said to retrieve the crown from Grisedale Tarn and carry it down to Dunmail Raise in the hope that their king will rise again. With Dyfnwal's spear, they strike the topmost stone of the cairn and eventually, from deep within its heart, a disembodied voice replies: 'Not yet, not yet; wait awhile, my warriors.'

While it is fascinating to wonder whether the ghostly visitors are themselves spooked by this experience, the main question is: was Dyfnwal a real-life character? It seems that he was, although he didn't meet his end at this spot. In his book *Strathclyde and the Anglo-Saxons in the Viking Age*, historian Tim Clarkson reveals that Dyfnwal (in Old English, *Dunmail*) was a 10th-century king of Strathclyde. With its capital at Govan, the kingdom of Strathclyde was one of the early medieval kingdoms of the

Britons; extending southwards into parts of modern-day England, it was also known as Cumberland and Cumbria. (This is the origin of the county name.)

Medieval chronicles confirm that Dyfnwal's territory was invaded by Edmund I of England in AD 945, and that in the ensuing battle he was defeated. Contrary to tradition, he survived and was allowed to retain his title, but he was forced to recognise the supremacy of Edmund I who leased the lands of Strathclyde to Máel Coluim, King of Alba, in a pact of allegiance. It is recorded that two of Dyfnwal's sons were deliberately blinded, but he had another son to whom he later abdicated his role. Dyfnwal died in 975, while on a pilgrimage to Rome.

While it has yet to reveal any human remains, Dunmail Raise may still mark the site of an ancient battle … or, more prosaically, it may be a boundary marker between the old counties of Westmorland and Cumberland. The legend itself is impossible to date, and it has been reinterpreted and embellished by generations of authors and poets. In his novel *Thorstein of the Mere* (1895), W.G. Collingwood describes how Dyfnwal (which he spells Domhnaill) flees from the Saxon armies and

Here, according to legend, lies the last king of Cumberland.

encounters a fairy woman sitting under a hawthorn tree. She leads him up a roaring stream to Grisedale Tarn and casts his crown into the water. Domhnaill is seen no more, but the place is 'still haunted, they say, by the fleeing king and the fairy maid flitting before him'.

The Lakeland poet William Wordsworth, who often walked that way himself, depicts a waggoner trudging patiently up the high pass with his horses while a summer storm is brewing:

> The horses cautiously pursue
> Their way, without mishap or fault;
> And now have reached that pile of stones,
> Heaped over brave King Dunmail's bones;
> He who had once supreme command,
> Last king of rocky Cumberland;
> His bones, and those of all his Power
> Slain here in a disastrous hour!

> (*The Waggoner*, 1819)

In his poem 'King Dunmail', John Pagen White imagines a stone being added to the cairn every year by an unseen sentinel, marking time until the king awakes:

> And when the Raise has reached its sum,
> Again will brave King Dunmail come;
> And all his Warriors marching down
> The dell, bear back his golden crown.

> And Dunmail, mantled, crowned, and mailed,
> Again shall Cumbria's King be hailed;
> And o'er his hills and valleys reign
> When Eildon's heights are field and plain.

> ('King Dunmail', from *Lays and Legends of the English Lake Country*, 1873)

ULLSWATER AND AIRA FORCE

The second largest of the English Lakes, Ullswater stretches in a ragged ribbon for about 9 miles (14.5km) from the high fells of Helvellyn to the softer landscape of the Eden Valley. On its eastern shore, the Aira Beck rises on a fell called Stybarrow Dodd and flows for a distance of about 4 miles (6.5km) before entering a steep-sided ravine, where it tumbles headlong towards Ullswater in an elegant white veil called Aira Force.

Since at least the mid-19th century, this 65-foot (20-metre) waterfall has been connected with the sad story of Lady Emma and her gallant suitor, a knight called Sir Eglamore. The lovers used to meet in a holly bower beside Aira Force. They were devoted to each other, but Sir Eglamore had a restless nature and a thirst for fame, which spurred him to travel far and wide in foreign lands, testing his skills in honourable combat. As Lady Emma waited disconsolately for his return, she started walking in her sleep. Every night she would ascend to the top of the waterfall, dropping handfuls of leaves into the raging water.

When Sir Eglamore returned and heard about Lady Emma's habit, he climbed up there in the darkness, hoping to surprise her. He beheld a silent, white-robed figure walking towards the top of the falls and reached out to wake her, but his touch startled her so much that she fell into the abyss with a scream of terror and was swept downwards with the force of the water.

In desperation, Sir Eglamore pulled her from the pool at the bottom and held her in his arms, declaring his eternal love; Lady Emma had time to murmur her own devotion before she died.

Stricken with remorse, Sir Eglamore built himself a hermit's cell on the shore, where he spent the rest of his life in mourning.

William Wordsworth, whose poetic heartstrings were always plucked by Cumbria's lakes and fells, immortalised this tragic tale in a poem entitled *The Somnambulist*. In the form of verse, he explains that Lady Emma's home stood on the site of Lyulph's Tower, which does actually exist: it is a castellated hunting lodge on the shore of Ullswater. However, it was built for the Duke of Norfolk in the late 1700s, long after the medieval age of chivalry in which the story is set. In fact, in his introductory notes Wordsworth makes it quite clear that he himself made up the entire story of Lady Emma and Sir Eglamore, after hearing from a friend, who was staying in Lyulph's Tower, that a young woman in the house was prone to sleepwalking and had been heard to scream as she reached the front door.

> Soul-shattered was the Knight, nor knew
> If Emma's Ghost it were,
> Or boding Shade, or if the Maid
> Her very self stood there.
> He touched; what followed who shall tell?
> The soft touch snapped the thread
> Of slumber – shrieking back she fell,
> And the Stream whirled her down the dell
> Along its foaming bed.

(William Wordsworth, *The Somnambulist*, 1835)

And it is to Ullswater that we owe one of Wordsworth's most iconic poems. In April 1802 he and his sister Dorothy were walking in the woods around Aira Force when they encountered a breathtaking sight. Daffodils were blooming in a great golden drift by the shore of the lake, and they stood and looked at them in wonder. In her journal, Dorothy recalled: '... we saw that there was a long belt of them along the shore, about the breadth of a country turnpike road. I never saw daffodils so beautiful. They grew among the mossy stones about and above them; some rested their heads upon these stones, as on a pillow, for weariness; and the rest tossed and reeled and danced, and seemed as if they verily laughed with the wind, that blew upon them over the lake; they looked so gay, ever glancing, ever changing.' (*Journals of Dorothy Wordsworth*, Vol. I, 1904.)

The sight lifted William Wordsworth's spirits, and he captured the scene in a memorable poem:

> I wandered lonely as a cloud
> That floats on high o'er vales and hills,
> When all at once I saw a crowd,
> A host, of golden daffodils;
> Beside the lake, beneath the trees,
> Fluttering and dancing in the breeze.
>
> Continuous as the stars that shine
> And twinkle on the milky way,
> They stretched in never-ending line
> Along the margin of a bay:
> Ten thousand saw I at a glance,
> Tossing their heads in sprightly dance.
>
> The waves beside them danced; but they
> Out-did the sparkling waves in glee:
> A poet could not but be gay,
> In such a jocund company:

I gazed – and gazed – but little thought
What wealth the show to me had brought:

For oft, when on my couch I lie
In vacant or in pensive mood,
They flash upon that inward eye
Which is the bliss of solitude;
And then my heart with pleasure fills,
And dances with the daffodils.

('I Wandered Lonely as a Cloud', 1807)

HELL'S KETTLES

A few miles south of Darlington in County Durham, in a field
beside a busy A-road, lie two small pools. They look nothing out
of the ordinary, except that one appears to be a slightly different
colour from the other. But the existence of these pools, which go
by the rather ominous-sounding name of Hell Kettles or Hell's
Kettles, can be traced precisely back to the year 1179, when a
quite extraordinary event is said to have taken place. The 16th-
century chronicler Raphael Holinshed explained:

> The king [Henry II] this yeare held his Christmasse at
> Winchester, at which time newes came abroad of a great
> wonder that had chanced at a place called Oxenhale,
> within the lordship of Derlington, in which place a part
> of the earth lifted itself up on high in appearance like to
> a mightie tower, and so it remained from nine of the
> clocke in the morning, till the even tide, and then it fell

downe with an horrible noise, so that as much as were thereabout, were put in a great feare. That péece of earth with the fall was swallowed up, leaving a great déepe pit in the place, as was to be seene many yeares after.

(*Chronicles of England*, 1st ed., 1577)

Stripped of some of its melodrama, this is an event that modern-day geologists would describe as 'catastrophic subsidence'. The underlying rocks include deposits of gypsum which can dissolve rapidly under certain conditions, resulting in the collapse of surface layers and the sudden appearance of sinkholes. But in the 12th century, this phenomenon was ascribed to the work of dark forces and it wasn't long before the pools were called the Kettles of Hell or the Devil's Kettles.

As to the properties of the pools, imaginations ran riot. A belief sprang up that they were bottomless, and the saying 'as deep as Hell's Kettles' was applied to anything immeasurably deep. It was said that their turbulent, sulphurous waters – or the enormous pike and eels that infested them – had claimed the lives of humans and cattle, whose spirits could sometimes be heard shrieking in anguish. These victims included a local farmer who refused to pause in his harvesting to honour St Barnabas' Day (11 June). When challenged, he shouted defiantly: 'Barnaby yea! Barnaby nay! A cartload of hay, whether God will or nay!' Immediately, he was swallowed up into one of the pools, together with his cart and horses. Long afterwards, pious observers claimed that they could still be seen floating, many fathoms deep.

Originally, there were four Hell's Kettles, but one has since been filled in and two of the remaining three have joined together. While the larger pool is filled with run-off rainwater, the other, known as Croft Kettle, is fed by clear subterranean springs that filter through limestone, and it supports plant species that are more usually found in the fens of East Anglia. For this reason, the pools are classed as a Site of Special Scientific Interest.

In the 1500s, there was a local belief that Hell's Kettles were connected to the River Tees, and such was their fame that King Henry VIII sent an inspector to see whether this was true. By way of an experiment, the inspector had the dubious idea of painting a cross on a duck and placing it on one of the pools. The bird is said to have been sucked down by the water and was later found swimming by the Croft bridge, where the River Skerne joins the Tees. How it got there is a matter for debate, but it seems more likely that it chose to travel above rather than below ground. A man was later tasked with diving down to see if he could solve the puzzle. He, too, is said to have miraculously emerged in the River Skerne.

These fanciful stories about Hell's Kettles, and their reputation for transporting a creature – or even a person – through a watery tunnel into another world, must have been known to a young lad called Charles Dodgson, who grew up at the nearby village of Croft on Tees. In later years, using the pen name of Lewis Carroll, he wrote his famous children's story, *Alice's Adventures in Wonderland* (1865). It is thought that Hell's Kettles gave him the idea for Alice's journey down the rabbit hole: 'Down, down, down. Would the fall *never* come to an end! "I wonder how many miles I've fallen by this time?" she said aloud. "I must be getting somewhere near the centre of the earth."'

BAMBURGH CASTLE

The King is gone from Bambrough castle:
Long may the Princess mourn,
Long may she stand on the castle wall,
Looking for his return.

(Trad. ballad credited to Robert Lambe, from William
Hutchinson's *A View of Northumberland*, 1778)

Occupying a rocky outcrop that rises above the pounding waves of
the North Sea, Bamburgh Castle in Northumberland looks
brooding and impregnable, its massive towers ready to face down
any adversary, whether they are advancing from the sea or the sky.
But long ago it was a foe within its very walls that nearly brought
about the downfall of its king.

In the 6th century, the Anglian kingdom of Bernicia was ruled
by the wonderfully named Ida the Flame-bearer, whose fortress
stood on Bamburgh's rocky plateau. Folklore tells how King Ida
was a widower who remarried and brought his bride home to
meet his 18-year-old daughter, Margaret. The king was so
besotted with his new wife that he failed to notice her jealousy.
Unwisely, he boasted that Margaret's beauty exceeded that of any
other woman, and his wife, who was a witch, began to plot
Margaret's doom.

By sunset the next day the evil queen had transformed
Margaret into a fearsome dragon, which became known as the
Laidley Worm. In Northumbrian dialect 'laidley' means 'loathly'
or 'loathsome', while the Old English 'wyrm' or 'worm' was used

to describe a serpent or dragon. The creature terrorised the neighbourhood and her breath was so venomous that no grass or crops would grow for many miles around. Such was her appetite that every day she drank the milk of seven cows, which was poured for her into a stone trough.

The Laidley Worm's fearsome reputation spread to a far shore and reached the ears of a young man named Childe* of Wynd, who was the son of King Ida. Realising that his sister was in trouble, he assembled his followers and constructed a ship from rowan wood, which offered protection against evil spells. Then he set sail for Bamburgh.

On seeing his ship, the queen sent some accomplices (described as 'witch-wives') to sink it, but they were driven back by the rowan's powerful magic. Leaping ashore, Childe of Wynd was confronted by the Laidley Worm and he drew his sword, threatening to strike her dead. The dragon responded:

> Oh! Quit thy sword, and bend thy bow,
> And give me kisses three;
> For though I am a poisonous worm,
> No hurt will I do to thee.

Recognising his sister's voice, Childe bravely kissed the dragon three times; instantly, the spell was broken, the creature vanished and Margaret was standing before him. Together they ran towards the castle carrying branches of rowan, which they used to turn the evil queen into a toad. She waddled away into a cave, but would occasionally emerge to spit venom onto anyone who

* Childe is an archaic term for a noble youth, yet to achieve knighthood.

crossed her path; meanwhile, the king rejoiced at being reunited with his children.

The story of The Laidley Worm of Spindleston Heugh was told in a ballad by Robert Lambe, an 18th-century vicar of Norham. Lambe claimed that the ballad was 500 years old and attributed it to an 'old Mountain Bard' named Duncan Frasier, who lived in the Cheviot Hills, but some historians suspect that Lambe himself composed it.

Spindleston Heugh refers to the low hills or 'heughs' near Spindleston, a couple of miles from Bamburgh, where the Laidley Worm is said to have lurked. Until the late 1800s, Ordnance Survey maps marked the position of a rectangular stone known as 'the Laidley Worm's trough', from which the creature was said to drink.

While King Ida plays a passive role in the story of the Laidley Worm, another legend portrays Bamburgh as the stronghold of a true romantic hero: Sir Lancelot, a knight of King Arthur. In Arthurian legend, a fortress called Dolorous Gard had fallen under a sinister enchantment before Sir Lancelot broke through its defences and captured it, whereupon he renamed it Joyous Gard.

The 'gard' element may derive from Din Guayrdi – a fortress of the Iron Age Britons mentioned in Nennius' *History of the Britons* (c. 830), and believed to be an old name for Bamburgh. Sir Thomas Malory offers two castles as the location of Joyous Gard: 'Some men say it was Anwick [Alnwick] and some men say it was Bamborow [Bamburgh].' (*Le Morte d'Arthur*, c. 1470, ed. Sir Edward Strachey, 1868.)

It was at Joyous Gard that Sir Lancelot offered temporary refuge to the fleeing lovers, Tristan and Isolde, who were being pursued by Isolde's husband, King Mark of Cornwall: 'And so Sir Launcelot brought Sir Tristram [Tristan] and La Beale Isoud [the beautiful Isolde] unto Joyous Gard, that was his own castle that he had won with his own hands ... and wit ye well that castle was garnished and furnished for a king and a queen royal there to have sojourned.'

Later, when Sir Lancelot embroiled himself in an affair with Queen Guinevere, the wife of King Arthur, Guinevere was condemned to be burnt at the stake for treason. At the last minute, Sir Lancelot whisked her to safety: 'And so he rode his way with the queen ... unto Joyous Gard, and there he kept her as a noble knight should do ....'

At the end of the tragic tale, when King Arthur has been slain by Mordred and Queen Guinevere has died in a nunnery, Sir Lancelot succumbs to sorrow. According to his wish, his body is taken to Joyous Gard in a procession lit by a hundred torches: 'And there they laid his corpse in the body of the quire, and sang and read many psalters and prayers over him and about him.'

WALES

CANTRE'R GWAELOD
(THE LOWLAND HUNDRED)

'The sleepers of Gwaelod,' said Elphin, 'they who
sleep in peace and security, trusting to the vigilance
of Seithenyn, what will become of them?'

(Thomas Love Peacock, *The Misfortunes of Elphin*, 1829)

Cardigan Bay (Bae Ceredigion) takes a generous bite out of the
coastline of Wales, its fine sandy beaches and gorse-topped
headlands sweeping in a long curve from the Llŷn peninsula right
down to Strumble Head in Pembrokeshire. Looking due west, the
nearest landmass is Ireland ... but according to an old legend, this
wasn't always the case.

Thousands of years ago, so it is said, dry land extended for
many miles to the west, and on it were built 16 noble cities.
Their streets bustled with traders, and all around them was
fertile farmland and forest. This prosperous country was called
Maes Gwyddno ('the plain of Gwyddno') after its king,
Gwyddno Garanhir.

To protect this low-lying kingdom from the sea, it was
encircled by embankments with sluice gates which were closed at
high tide and opened again when the waves receded; this system
depended on the constant vigilance of watchmen who took turns
to patrol the banks. But disaster was about to strike. One night,
with a storm brewing out at sea, a watchman called Seithenyn was

partying and forgot to close the gates. As he lay in a drunken stupor, enormous waves crashed through on the high tide and the entire kingdom was submerged.

> *Seithenhin saw de allan.*
> *ac edrychuir de varanres*
> *mor. maes guitnev ry toes.*
>
> 'Seithenyn, stand and come out
> and look at the fury
> of the sea. It has covered Maes Gwyddno.'
>
> (From an anonymous poem, 'Boddi Maes Gwyddno',
> 'The Drowning of the Land of Gwyddno',
> *The Black Book of Carmarthen,* c. 1250)

An alternative version of the story blames a young woman, Mererid, who was in charge of the floodgates and was seduced by Seithenyn on the fateful night. But it is Seithenyn who has the dubious honour of being listed in the medieval Welsh Triads manuscripts as one of the Three Immortal Drunkards of the Isle of Britain.

Forever afterwards, the submerged land was known as Cantre'r Gwaelod, the Lowland Hundred (a *cantref* or 'hundred' being an old term for an administrative region). Although most of the inhabitants drowned, it was said that a lucky few escaped, among them Gwyddno, Seithenyn and their families; they ran east along one of the three causeways to higher ground. Saint Tudno, whose church lies above the town of Llandudno, is traditionally named as one of Seithenyn's sons, having pledged himself to a life of religious devotion to atone for his father's neglect.

As the story was handed from one generation to the next, eager observers occasionally caught tantalising glimpses of ruined buildings, either exposed far offshore at low tide or shimmering up through the clear water. The bells of lost churches were heard ringing when the sea was calm, a phenomenon which inspired the popular 19th-century song 'Clychau Aberdyfi' ('The Bells of Aberdovey').

So was Cantre'r Gwaelod a real place, and did the disaster really happen? In his *Topographical Dictionary of Wales* (1833), Samuel Lewis claimed that 'in the sea, about seven miles to the west of Aberystwith, is a collection of loose stones, termed Caer Wyddno, the fort or palace of Gwyddno; and adjoining to it are vestiges of what is supposed to have been the southern embankment of Cantrev Gwaelod'. He suggested that the inundation happened around AD 500.

Lewis's 'palace of Gwyddno' has yet to be found, but there is other fascinating evidence that may point to some kernel of truth in the legend. Off the Welsh coast, extremely low tides have long been exposing whole forests of ancient tree stumps, blackened and still rooted in layers of peat. In the 19th century they were sometimes dug up by local people and used as gateposts. In recent years the trees have been identified as willow, hazel, oak, pine and birch; carbon dating shows that they were growing here between 3,100 and 4,000 years ago. Intriguingly, human footprints have also been preserved, along with the remains of red deer, brown bear and aurochs.

At various points around Cardigan Bay (Bae Ceredigion), three low shingle ridges running out to sea are also revealed at low tide. These were always known as the causeways (*sarnau*) that led to Cantre'r Gwaelod, and were the routes by which the survivors escaped. It has since been proven that they are glacial features, but in 2014 archaeologists discovered stretches of a man-made timber walkway which dates back at least to the Bronze Age.

> *Intriguingly, human footprints have also been preserved.*

While there is no historical evidence to suggest a sudden inundation in the 6th century, the legend may recall an older and more gradual process. Scientists can estimate the rate at which sea levels rose after the last glacial period; from about 8,000 years ago, the land that is now Cardigan Bay was beginning to be swallowed by the sea and any human settlers would have had to cope with an increasingly waterlogged environment. And maybe – just maybe

– a storm coincided with a tidal surge that devastated an already precarious settlement. In his book *Sunken Cities* (1957), the geologist Dr F.J. North wonders whether legends such as Cantre'r Gwaelod represent a kind of inherited memory, preserving the earliest records of human experience in what is now Britain.

Meanwhile, in Aberdyfi, the ghostly peals of the Lowland Hundred can still be heard. Beneath the jetty, sculptor Marcus Vergette has fixed a 'Time and Tide Bell', which is rung naturally by the sea at high tide. The sound invokes a nostalgia for lands lost, and reminds us of our own predicament as sea levels continue to rise.

LLYN Y FAN FACH

One summer day in a century long ago, a farmer's son was sitting and watching over his cattle as they grazed by a lake called Llyn y Fan Fach, high above the village of Llanddeusant in South Wales. The weather was warm and as the sun glimmered on the water the young man was astonished to see a beautiful woman, apparently sitting on its surface and combing her hair while admiring her own reflection.

He scrambled to his feet and held out his hand, offering her a share of his barley-bread and cheese in the hope that she would come closer. But the woman admonished him: '*Cras dy fara; nid hawdd fy nala!*' ('Hard-baked is thy bread; 'tis not easy to catch me!') Then she dived away into the lake.

That night, the young man sought his mother's advice and she suggested that he offer some unbaked dough instead. Next morning, he went up to the lake and waited for the vision to appear. But the lake-maiden's disgust was even greater and before she plunged away she shouted: '*Llaith dy fara! Ti ni fynna!*' ('Unbaked is thy bread! I will not have thee!') At his wits' end, and possibly suspecting that he'd fallen into a medieval version of *The Great British Bake Off*, on the third morning the young man took up some half-baked bread and was relieved to find that it was exactly to the lake-maiden's liking. He begged her to marry him and to his joy she agreed.

But, of course, there was a catch. The woman slipped away and sank beneath the waves; seconds later a grey-haired, noble-looking man rose up from the water, accompanied by two young women – both of whom looked identical to the lake-maiden. 'These are my daughters,' he told the young man. 'Choose the correct one, and you may have her hand in marriage, together with a dowry of as many cattle and sheep as she can count in a single breath.'

The young man was confused, but one of the women edged her foot surreptitiously forwards. Taking it as a sign, he successfully identified her as his betrothed and they were married soon afterwards. There was, however, a condition to their marriage, to which he readily agreed because it seemed so unlikely: if he struck her three times, at the third blow she would leave him and take all her animals with her.

The couple went to live at a farm called Esgair Llaethdy, where they had three handsome sons. But then the unthinkable happened: at a christening, and at a funeral, and lastly in jest, the farmer dealt his wife a playful or consoling pat, and at the third gesture she bade him farewell and set out towards the lake, calling all her livestock to follow her. They all disappeared beneath the surface, leaving behind only the furrow of the plough that the oxen were still pulling. The desperate farmer threw himself into the water to try and bring them back, but drowned in the attempt.

When they grew up, the farmer's sons often visited Llyn y Fan Fach in the hope of meeting their mother and they were overjoyed when she finally appeared to them. Their role in life, she told them, was to heal the sick, and she showed them where to gather medicinal herbs. They followed her advice and became renowned healers, and their wisdom passed from one generation to the next. Such was their fame that even in the 18th century there were local families claiming direct descent from 'the Physicians of Myddfai'.

The 14th-century Welsh manuscript known as *The Red Book of Hergest* contains a compilation of 188 prescriptions said to have been

> *Perhaps the sparkling blue waters of Llyn y Fan Fach still hold memories of the beguiling nymph and her husband.*

collected directly from the famous physicians. These were translated by John Williams, Rector of Llanymawddwy, in 1861. Some sound like natural herbal remedies, while others have a distinct whiff of old magic: 'For deafness: Take some elm rods and lay them upon the embers, then receive the water that exudes from the rods in a clean vessel, and get the oil of a black eel, and as much honey, and as much juice of betony, mix them together,

drop into the ear and plug with the wool of a black lamb.'
(*Meddygon Myddvai*, trans. Rev. John Williams, 1861.)

Williams explains that a man called Rhiwallon and his sons Cadwgan, Gruffydd and Einion all became physicians to Rhys Gryg, Lord of Llandovery and Dinefwr Castles, who gave them lands and privileges so that they could help poor people who were most in need.

In folklore, there are many stories of humans who encounter mysterious lake-dwellers; usually, the human is carried off into the depths, never to be seen again. In his treatise *A Book on Nymphs, Sylphs, Pygmies, and Salamanders, and on the Other Spirits*, the 16th-century philosopher Paracelsus explained that nymphs – the elemental spirits of water – long to marry humans because in doing so they acquire a soul, and this quality is passed to their children. He warns: '… one who has a nymph for a wife, should not let her get close to any water, or at least should not offend her while they are on water … But they are so much obliged to man and so closely bound to him, that they cannot get away from him, unless there is a reason for it, and this happens at the place from which they come.' (*Four treatises of Theophrastus von Hohenheim, called Paracelsus,* ed. H. E. Sigerist, 1941.)

Perhaps the sparkling blue waters of Llyn y Fan Fach still hold memories of the beguiling nymph and her husband, and the talented healers who sprang from them. John Williams observes that the late Rice Williams, MD, of Aberystwyth, who died in 1842, 'appears to have been the last, although not the least eminent, of the Physicians descended from the mysterious Lady of Llyn-y-Fan'.

BARDSEY ISLAND

... there is an Island neere unto Wales, called Insula
Bardorum, and Bardsey, whereof the one name in
Latine, and the other in Saxon or old English, signifieth
the Island of the Bardes or Barthes.

(Raphael Holinshed, *Chronicles*, 2nd ed. 1587)

Just one and a half miles (2.4km) long and half a mile (0.8km)
wide, the island of Bardsey (in Welsh, *Ynys Enlli*) lies off the tip of
the Llŷn Peninsula in North Wales. Its single rounded hill, known
as Bardsey Mountain, rises to nearly 550 feet (168 metres) and
tapers into a tail of low-lying grassland where cattle graze.

Saint Cadfan, an early Christian missionary-saint, may have
been seeking solitude and space when he founded a monastic
settlement here in the 6th century. But Bardsey's reputation as a
holy isle began to spread: Saint Cadfan was buried here, together
with Saint Beuno, the uncle of Saint Winefride. Saint Dyfrig,
who reputedly crowned King Arthur, retired to Bardsey and died
here. Within a few centuries, the belief had sprung up that three
pilgrimages to Bardsey were equal to one pilgrimage to Rome and
thousands of hopeful travellers were bending their steps towards
'the island of 20,000 saints'.

Twenty thousand saints, all buried on Bardsey? It's hard to
imagine, but maybe this claim was never meant to be taken
literally. In the 17th century the clergyman Thomas Fuller had a
similar thought when he wrote: 'Where would so many thousand

bodies find graves in so petty an islet? But I retrench myself, confessing it more facile to find graves in Berdsey for so many saints, than saints for so many graves.' (*The History of the Worthies of England*, 1662.)

Attempting to account for part of the saintly influx, Evan Richard writes in The Cambrian Register (Vol. III, 1818) that 900 monks fled to Bardsey when a King of Northumberland attacked their monastery at Bangor-is-y-coed in Flintshire and massacred 1,200 of their brethren. He explains that there were two burial grounds – one for the saints and one for the common people – and adds that 'the whole island is full of dead men's bones', to the extent that milk and butter would curdle if kept too near to the graveyard. Perhaps he was exaggerating ... but during the 19th century, when more than 100 people were living on Bardsey, they dug up so many bones that they used them to make fences.

There is an enduring belief that Merlin's grave is on the island.

Evan Richard lists the notable figures who he claims are buried on Bardsey, among them 'Myrddin ap Morfryn (or Merlinus Caledonius, or Sylvestris)' – in other words, Merlin, the magician of Arthurian legend. An old Welsh story tells how Merlin fell in love with an evil sorceress named Nimue, who did not kill him but trapped him in a cave (or alternatively in a case of glass) on the island. With him, it is said, are the Thirteen Treasures of Britain and the true throne of the realm.

There is still an enduring belief that Merlin's grave is

somewhere on the island, and his name has been given to a unique variety of apple tree that flourishes in Bardsey's wet and windy climate. 'Merlin's apple' has been growing here for centuries, and may be a descendant of trees tended by medieval monks. The link with King Arthur's last resting place of Avalon, the 'Isle of Apples' with its promise of eternal life, is irresistible, as is the fact that choughs – scarlet-beaked members of the crow family – breed on Bardsey: according to legend, these are the birds in which King Arthur's spirit is reincarnated.

Although there is no archaeological evidence of the earliest chapel on Bardsey, the remains of a 13th-century Augustinian abbey can still be seen. A monastic community survived here until the mid-1500s, when Henry VIII's fallout with the Catholic Church in Rome led him to dissolve all the monasteries in England and Wales. The ruined monastery then became a useful haven for smugglers. But Bardsey's holiness was still preserved: in 1773, when the traveller Thomas Pennant was taken there by local boatmen, he noted that 'the mariners seemed tinctured with the piety of the place; for they had not rowed far before they made a full stop, pulled off their hats and offered up a short prayer'. (*A Tour in Wales*, 1778.)

The population of Bardsey has waxed and waned over time. In the early 1900s there were about 100 inhabitants and a small school, and there was also a curious tradition, a century or more old, of electing and crowning a king of the island. However, in 1925, the king and most of the other islanders chose to seek new lives on the mainland. Nowadays there is a summer population of about 11, which is reduced to three or four during the winter.

On the Welsh mainland, the old pilgrimage routes to Bardsey were punctuated by resting places at holy wells, and under an age-old obligation a farmhouse at Nefyn used to offer a free meal to travellers. Modern-day pilgrims still enjoy an exhilarating sense of freedom and escape, but the sea crossing is notoriously tricky and they run a real risk of being marooned on the island, should the weather turn bad; not for nothing is it called Enlli, from the Welsh *yn y llif* or 'in the flood tide'.

> We slide in on an oiled keel,
> step ashore with birth-wet, wind-red faces
> wiping the salt from our eyes
> and notice sudden, welling
> quiet, and how here the breeze
> lets smells of growing things
> settle and grow warm, a host of presences
> drowsing, their wings too fine to see.

(Christine Evans, 'Enlli', *Selected Poems*, 2003)

CADAIR IDRIS

Cadair Idris (sometimes spelt Cader Idris) rises to a height of 2,930 feet (893 metres) above the town of Dolgellau in the Eryri (Snowdonia) National Park. Its name translates as 'the chair of Idris' and in legend its occupant was a giant who would throw boulders when he was in a rage; a group of rocks next to Llyn y Tri Graienyn, 'the lake of three pebbles', were shaken out of his shoe while he was striding across the mountain. But Idris had other talents: he was a prophet and a poet, and he was one of the three *Gwyn Serenyddion* or sublime astronomers of Wales, surveying the night sky from his observatory on the summit. Humans who felt tempted to join him were warned of the repercussions: it was said that if you spent a night on Cadair Idris you would either wake up as a brilliant poet or lose your mind – or you wouldn't wake up at all.

To make the risks even more exciting, Cadair Idris was said to be patrolled by Gwyn ap Nudd, another of the sublime astronomers, who was the ruler of the Otherworld; he was said to ride out on stormy nights, leading his pack of spectral hounds known as the Cŵn Annwn. This is one version of the Wild Hunt, a terrifying phenomenon of howling dogs and other predatory animals that scoured the sky in search of lost souls. To hear them was a warning of imminent death.

These spine-tingling stories attracted so many visitors to Cadair Idris, especially in the 19th century, that local people offered themselves for hire as mountain guides; a stone bothy near the summit provided temporary shelter if the weather turned bad (or if the Wild Hunt appeared over the horizon!). In 1871 the clergyman and diarist Francis Kilvert made the ascent with a local man, Mr Pugh, who had once won a wager that he couldn't climb Cadair Idris four times in one day. Kilvert and Pugh enjoyed a few seconds of clear visibility before driving rain forced them into the bothy – where they fortified themselves with boiled eggs and bread and butter, washed down with spring water.

Obviously hoping for a more haunting experience, the poet

Felicia Hemans spent a night up there on her own. She described the resulting horrors in graphic detail:

> I lay there in silence,—a spirit came o'er me;
> Man's tongue hath no language to speak what I saw;
> Things glorious, unearthly, passed floating before me,
> And my heart almost fainted with rapture and awe.
> I viewed the dread beings around us that hover,
> Though veiled by the mists of mortality's breath;
> And I called upon darkness the vision to cover,
> For a strife was within me of madness and death.

('The Rock of Cader Idris', *Welsh Melodies*, 1822)

Anyone wishing to escape from the hounds of Gwyn ap Nudd might have been tempted to dive into the clear waters of Llyn Cau, a glacial lake on the south side of the mountain. But Llyn Cau has its own lurking dangers: according to one account, a dragon that was terrorising the local people was captured by King Arthur and released into the lake. A young man attempted to swim across the lake in the 18th century, but he was seized in the monster's jaws and disappeared.

King Arthur has another connection with Cadair Idris, as he is said to have sat in the summit 'chair' to survey his kingdom. The Flintshire-born poet Jane Brereton was probably aware of this connection when she composed *Merlin: A Poem* in honour of Queen Caroline, the wife of King George II. In the poem, Merlin appears to Brereton in a dream and gives her a message for the queen. He reminds her of all his great deeds, and tells her:

> To Cader Ydris oft I took my Way;
> Rose with the Sun, toil'd up th' Ascent all Day;
> But scarce could reach the Mountains tow'ring height,
> E'er Radiant Vesper usher'd in the Night.

> (*Merlin: A Poem*, 1735)

If Cadair Idris was an arduous climb for Merlin, it was a pleasant weekly stroll for the daring parishioners of Llanfihangel-y-Pennant and Ystrad Gwyn, who – according to tradition – got together every Sunday and gambled beneath a crag known as 'The Rock of the Evil One'. This feature was so called because the Devil once joined them, and when he won he danced jubilantly on the top, leaving his hoof prints behind.

Regardless of its dark stories, Cadair Idris continues to draw climbers who are eager to admire its sweeping views right down to the blue curve of Cardigan Bay (Bae Ceredigion). In ages past, it must have made an excellent lookout point. The traditional Welsh song 'Men of Harlech' is said to refer to a siege of nearby Harlech Castle by English soldiers in the 15th century; a regimental version of the lyrics describes a beacon which has been lit on the mountain to warn of imminent attack:

> Tongues of fire on Idris flaring,
> News of foemen near declaring,
> To heroic deeds of daring,
> Call you, Harlech men.

CWM IDWAL

Llyn Idwal (Idwal's Lake) lies at an altitude of about 1,220 feet (370 metres) in Eryri (Snowdonia), North Wales. Looming over it to the west is the summit of Y Garn, while to the south rise the formidable peaks of Glyder Fawr and Glyder Fach.

With its pebbly shore and clear water, it seems remote and idyllic – a perfect place for stone-skimming or picnicking on a warm day. But when the traveller and writer Thomas Pennant came here in the late 1700s, his impressions were very different. He wrote: 'It is a fit place to inspire murderous thoughts, environed with horrible precipices ... The shepherds fable, that it is the haunt of Daemons; and that no bird dare fly over its damned water, fatal as that of Avernus.'* (*A Tour in Wales*, 1778.)

Pennant wasn't necessarily setting the best precedent for local tourism, but he had heard the folklore about Llyn Idwal and was obviously expecting it to live up to its reputation. An old story tells how, in the 12th century, one of the sons of Owain, Prince of Gwynedd was murdered here by his jealous uncle, Nefydd Hardd (Nefydd the Handsome), who had been charged with his welfare.

Idwal, so it is said, was a good-looking and clever young man, but he had no interest in following his father's example and becoming a warrior. In contrast, Rhun, the son of Nefydd Hardd, was dull and ignorant. Nefydd, who had been appointed the foster father of Idwal while Owain was away campaigning, took Rhun and Idwal for a walk by the lake and pushed Idwal into the water, laughing as he drowned. The lake that claimed Idwal's life also took his name – as did Cwm Idwal, the valley in which it lies.

In the early 19th century, the writer Peter Bayley developed the story of Idwal's murder into an epic poem in which Idwal falls in love with Hartslin, a beautiful young woman who is shipwrecked on the shore near his castle. Their romance ends in bloodshed and tragedy. Bayley suggests that Idwal may be buried on a small island in the lake, but he also offers alternative outcomes, including the notion that Idwal sailed with his brother, Madoc, to America:

---

* Lake Avernus, an extinct volcano in southern Italy, was considered by the Romans to be an entrance to the underworld, and by the Greeks to be the haunt of Hecate, goddess of witchcraft.

And yet there are, or were in th' olden time,
Who told that Idwal 'scaped the drowning tide:
That o'er the Atlantic waves, in other climes,
With Madoc did his brother long abide.
Some fable, too, that Idwal never died;
But that he lives beneath the enchanted lake,
The fairies' prize, and talisman, and pride,
And in Elysium sleeps; save when they wake
In summer nights, to sing, and dance, and merry make.

(*Idwal: A Poem*, 1824)

At the far end of Llyn Idwal, climbers heading for the summit of Glyder Fawr may choose to scramble up the wall of The Devil's Kitchen (in Welsh, *Y Twll Du*, or 'the black hole'). This is a natural cleft in a steep, dark rock face which can appear to 'smoke' in damp weather, as the moist air forms a plume of swirling cloud. The Devil is said to beckon weary travellers into his kitchen and they are never seen again.

Geologically speaking, Llyn Idwal sits in a corrie (in Welsh, *cwm*): a steep-sided, cup-shaped hollow. When Charles Darwin came here in the 1800s, he realised that Cwm Idwal had been shaped by the action of glaciers and correctly attributed some of the huge boulders to the work of moving ice. He also observed that the rocks contained the fossils of tiny marine creatures and concluded that they must have formed within an ancient ocean.

Modern-day geologists consider Cwm Idwal to be a textbook example of a glaciated valley because it contains so many features that can be attributed to the last Ice Age. It is strewn with glacial moraines, which are heaps of rocks and debris dumped by retreating ice. The largest of these is known as Bedd y Cawr (The Giant's Grave), and alternatively as Beddau Milwyr Ynys Prydain (The Graves of the Soldiers of the Island of Britain).

The latter name, commemorating the soldiers of Britain, may refer to a different incarnation of Idwal. A figure called Idwal Iwrch (Idwal the Roebuck) was the son of a 7th-century king of Gwynedd called Cadwaladr Fendigaid. Both Cadwaladr and Idwal exist only as brief notes in historical record, but Cadwaladr has become known in legend as the last King of Gwynedd to put up an armed resistance against the Anglo-Saxons.

Birds and wild flowers thrive in this seemingly inhospitable landscape. Ring ouzels and wheatears are among the summer migrants that nest here, and in high rock crevices the rare brwynddail y mynydd, or Snowdon lily (*Gagea serotina*), opens its delicate white flowers. Snowdonia hawkweed (*Hieracium snowdoniense*) is even more elusive: a species once believed to be extinct, it was rediscovered in Cwm Idwal in 2002.

DINAS BRÂN

In the medieval Welsh texts collectively known as the *Mabinogion*, a legend tells how Brân the Blessed, a giant warrior-hero and king of Britain, was visited by Matholwch, a king of Ireland. Matholwch sought the hand of Brân's sister, Branwen, in marriage. Brân gave his consent, but shortly after the wedding his troublesome half-brother, Efnisien, appeared and was outraged

that he had not been consulted too. He wounded Matholwch's horses as a deliberate insult, which enraged Matholwch so much that, once back in Ireland, he treated Branwen like a servant and deprived her of all contact with her family.

In desperation, Branwen tamed a starling and taught it to speak; she told it how to recognise her brother and sent it across the Irish Sea with a message begging him to rescue her. Immediately, Brân gathered a huge army and set sail for Ireland. In the ensuing battle, most of his men were killed and Brân himself was struck with a poisoned arrow.

Branwen and a handful of survivors escaped with the dying Brân, who commanded them to cut off his head and take it on a long journey around Britain before burying it on the White Mount in London. The men complied and it was said that Britain would suffer no threat from invasion while Brân's head lay in that spot, which is now the site of the Tower of London.

'Brân', in Welsh, means 'raven', and this could be the source of the superstition that the kingdom will fall if the ravens desert the Tower of London. Meanwhile, at Llangollen in North Wales, an ancient castle was said to be the seat of the legendary hero. It was known as Dinas Brân, meaning 'Brân's fortress'.

Brân has left no physical trace for mere mortals to discover, unless it is in the ravens that haunt the desolate moorland of nearby Mynydd Hiraethog. On the summit of Dinas Brân, humans left their imprint in the Iron Age with the construction of a hill fort. In the 8th century Elisedd ap Gwylog, a founder of the kingdom of Powys, is said to have had a stronghold here. Later, the Princes of Powys Fadog – the northern section of Powys –

built an impressive castle which guarded the natural route of any invaders from the east, along the Dee Valley into north-west Wales.

The princes' castle was completed around 1270, but its splendour was short-lived because in 1277 Edward I of England set about bringing the independent Welsh kingdoms under his rule. His formidable armies swept away any opposition through sheer force of numbers and one stronghold after another began to fall. Sensing defeat, the Welsh garrison at Dinas Brân abandoned the castle and set it alight, so that it could never be used by their enemies. Even the smouldering ruin impressed Henry de Lacy, Earl of Lincoln and Chief Councillor of Edward I; he urged the king to reinstate it, as he believed that there was no stronger castle either in Wales or England.

But the castle of Dinas Brân was never rebuilt, and in the centuries that followed its crumbling walls attracted dreamers and poets. In the 14th century, a bard named Hywel ab Einion penned an ode to a dark-eyed princess who had spurned his love: it was addressed to Myfanwy Fychan of Castell Dinas Brân. The original manuscript was found secreted in the stonework of the castle (an alternative story claims it was tucked into a nearby oak tree) and it is now preserved in the National Library of Wales.

Hywel's poem was translated by the 18th-century traveller Thomas Pennant in *A Tour in Wales* (1778). In turn, the words inspired John Ceiriog Hughes to compose the poem *Myfanwy Fychan*, which won him the Chair at the Llangollen Eisteddfod in 1858. Around the same time, Richard Davies wrote some lyrics which the composer Joseph Parry set to music:

Paham mae dicter, O Myfanwy,
Yn llenwi'th lygaid duon di?
A'th ruddiau tirion, O Myfanwy,
Heb wrido wrth fy ngweled i?

'Why so the anger, Oh Myfanwy,
That fills your dark eyes?
Your gentle cheeks, Oh Myfanwy,
No longer blush beholding me?'

('Myfanwy', 1875)

There is some mystery surrounding the original identity of Myfanwy Fychan, because she is said to have lived at Dinas Brân at a time when it was in ruin, but her name has been immortalised in one of the most iconic and enduring love songs of Wales.

It has long been believed that Dinas Brân is enchanted. According to folklore, a silver harp is buried beneath the hill, and only a boy and a white dog with a silver eye will ever be able to find it. Fairies or *Tylwyth Teg* are said to dance in a hollow known as Nant yr Ellyllon ('the valley of the elves'), and a story is told about a young shepherd named Tudur who stumbled across them. Their fiddler was a tiny man wearing a coat of birch leaves and a gorse flower for a cap; Tudur was invited to join in, but when he did so the fiddler turned into the Devil and Tudur found himself being whirled out of control. He was discovered next morning by his employer, still spinning dizzily in the hollow.

SCOTLAND

OSSIAN'S CAVE

It is an old legend, told around the firesides of Ireland and Scotland. Sometime in the 3rd century AD, Fionn Mac Cumhaill and his fighting-men, the Fianna, formed the bodyguard of the Irish High King, Cormac Mac Art. One evening, as Fionn and the Fianna were returning from a day's hunting in the hills, they chanced upon a fawn lying in the grass. Strangely, instead of running away, the creature allowed the men to approach. Even more strangely, the dogs licked and nuzzled it with great gentleness.

The fawn followed the hunters home to their fortress and later that evening, when Fionn was alone, a beautiful young woman, richly robed, appeared before him. She told him that her name was Sadbh, and she was the fawn he had encountered earlier. A druid, named Fear Doirche, had tried to seduce her and when she refused him he had retaliated by transforming her into a deer. She had lived in that state for three years, until she happened to meet a kind-hearted apprentice of Fear Doirche who told her that if she could enter the fortress of the Fianna she would regain her human form.

Fionn was enchanted with Sadbh and offered her the safety of his home for as long as she wished. The two became lovers and Sadbh fell pregnant, but the time came for Fionn and some of his warriors to go and fight off some invaders. When they returned, Sadbh was missing and Fionn questioned the men left behind. They told him that the worst had happened. Fionn's hunting horn had sounded, and an exact likeness of Fionn and his hounds had appeared before the fort. Before they could stop her, Sadbh had rushed out, eager to greet her love, but instead she was snatched up by Fear Doirche. She struggled, but he turned her back into a fawn; his dogs seized her and carried her away.

For 14 long years, Fionn grieved and searched for Sadbh, and whenever he went hunting he took only those dogs whom he trusted most, lest he encounter her again in deer form. One evening his hounds ran off to greet a stranger – a youth with long hair and fair features, who showed no fear. He told Fionn that he remembered living with his mother, a gentle hind who never left his side, but that a man had come and forced her to go away with him. Knowing full well that he was looking at his own son, Fionn took the youth into his care and named him Oisín or Ossian, meaning 'fawn'.

Here, time did not exist; Ossian never aged and all of his wishes were fulfilled.

Ossian grew up to become a skilled warrior; he could leap like a deer, and tread silently through any woodland. He was also a gifted poet, whom they called 'the sweet singer of the Fianna'. But one day, Ossian encountered a beautiful horsewoman called Niamh of the Golden Hair, daughter of the sea-god Manannán Mac Lir, who persuaded him to go with her to a blissful land called Tír na nÓg (or the Land of Youth). Here, time did not exist; Ossian never aged, and all of his wishes were fulfilled. Meanwhile, in the land that he had left behind, Fionn Mac Cumhaill and King Cormac died and a jealous new High King exterminated the Fianna in battle.

When Ossian began to yearn for another sight of his homeland, Niamh allowed him to go, on condition that he never dismounted from his horse. But when he got there and learned that Fionn and the Fianna were all dead, Ossian fell to the ground and the years caught up with him, turning him into an old man. He is said to have spent the last days of his life in the company of Saint Patrick, spurning his host's attempts to evangelise him, and composing mournful poetry about the age of freedom and glory that was lost.

> Alas! how sorrowful life's close;
> No hunting of the hind or stag,
> How different from my heart's desire!
> No trappings for our hounds, no hounds.
> Long are the clouds this night above me.
> No rising up to noble feats,
> No mirthful sport as we would wish,
> No swimming heroes in our lakes.

(Attributed to Ossian, from *The Book of the Dean of Lismore*, 16th century, compiled by James MacGregor, ed. Thomas McLaughlan, 1862)

In a vertical cliff face of Aonach Dubh, one of the Three Sisters of Glen Coe, is Ossian's Cave. According to folklore, this is where Sadbh gave birth to Ossian and in winter they roamed the surrounding hills – taking refuge, perhaps, in the Hidden Valley, which lies at the top of a narrow pass between the other 'Sisters', Beinn Fhada and Gearr Aonach.

Ossian's Cave has an entrance some 150 feet (46 metres) high, and a sloping, slippery floor. From the road that runs through the glen it is visible as a dark slit in the rock face, but it is accessible only to experienced climbers. The first recorded ascent was made in 1868 by Nicol Marquis, a shepherd who lived at Achtriochtan in Glen Coe.

Until about 1960 there was a Visitors' Book in the cave but, in his memoir *In High Places* (1972), the Scottish mountaineer Dougal Haston admitted to throwing it in jest at a party of rival climbers, and that it had been lost down the cliff. Haston went on to become a legend in his own right, being one of the first climbers (with Doug Scott) to summit Everest by the south-west face.

LOCH ETIVE

The sons of Uisnach came from Ireland and lived about
Loch Etive for a long time ....

(R. Angus Smith, *Loch Etive and the
Sons of Uisnach*, 1885)

From the wilds of Glen Etive, where a peaty river tumbles beneath
a succession of glowering crags, Loch Etive extends its long
crooked finger south-west towards the sea. This is a secretive loch,
difficult to access for much of its 20-mile (32km) length; steep
hills rise from its shores, fringed on the lower slopes with woods
of oak, hazel and alder. For two of the most famous lovers in Irish
legend, it offered the perfect place in which to hide.

The story begins in the ancient kingdom of Ulster, where the
king, Conchobar (Conor) Mac Nessa, held a feast in his hall. The
guests were entertained by the royal bard, whose wife was
pregnant. As a favour, the bard asked the king's druid to foretell
the child's future. The druid placed his hand on the woman's belly
and said: 'You will have a daughter, the most beautiful woman
Ireland has ever seen, with clear green eyes, red lips and wavy
golden hair. She will bring trouble to all who love her, and cause
slaughter among the warriors of Ulster.'

Because of this dire prediction, the warriors of Ulster wanted
to kill the child as soon as she was born, but instead Conchobar
had her raised in secret, intending to marry her himself so that no
other man would dare to look at her. Her name was Deirdre and

she was just as beautiful as the bard predicted. One day her foster-father killed a calf outside in the snow and a raven flew down to pick at the carcass. As she watched, Deirdre said: 'My true love will be a man of these colours: skin as white as the snow, cheeks flushed the colour of blood, and hair like a raven's wing.'

Before long, Deirdre encountered just such a man. One of the king's warriors, called Naoise Mac Uisneach (Naoise, son of Uisneach), was riding through the forest with his two brothers, Aindle and Ardan. Deirdre fell in love with Naoise on sight and tried to seduce him. Naoise knew who she was and resisted, but Deirdre put a *geas* ('moral bond') on him, so he was compelled to run away with her. Knowing their love was forbidden, the pair

fled across Ireland with Naoise's brothers and sailed to Alba where they found safe harbour in Loch Etive.

Deirdre and Naoise hunted and slept in the fertile glens, and built a fortress beside the loch. They were blissfully happy, but the King of Ulster sent messengers to lure them back. The night before their departure, Deirdre dreamed that a raven had flown from Ireland with three drops of honey in its beak; when it landed the drops fell and turned to blood. She was seized with dread, but, try as she might, she could not dissuade Naoise and his brothers from returning to their homeland.

As she sailed away from Loch Etive and its quiet glens, Deirdre's tearful song floated back across the water. Those who

heard her lament, which was long and beautiful, remembered her as Deirdre of the Sorrows.

> Glen Etive, O Glen Etive,
> There I raised my earliest house,
> Beautiful its woods on rising,
> When the sun fell on Glen Etive.

('Deirdre's Lament', trans. R. Angus Smith, *Loch Etive and the Sons of Uisnach*, 1885)

When they reached Ireland, Naoise and his brothers realised that they had been trapped. The king's druid conjured a great sea-tide and they swam against it until they were overcome with exhaustion, with Naoise valiantly carrying Deirdre on his shoulders. When the tide receded, Conchobar ordered his men to kill them; in a last gesture of honour, Naoise offered his own sword, which came from the sea-god Manannán Mac Lir. A warrior named Eoghan Mac Durthacht stepped forward and felled the three brothers with one blow.

Grief-stricken, Deirdre lived in Conchobar's court for a year and a day, repelling his attempts to seduce her. The king asked sarcastically if she hated any man more than he. 'Eoghan Mac Durthacht,' she replied, 'because he murdered my Naoise.' The king forced her into his chariot, intending to take her to Eoghan, but as they passed Naoise's grave Deirdre threw herself out and was killed instantly. It is said that two yew trees, symbolising immortality, grew up from the graves of Deirdre and Naoise, their roots intertwining as one.

Meanwhile, Conchobar's brutality divided the loyalty of his

men and precipitated a war in which hundreds of warriors died, including his own son. The prophecy of the bard, spoken before Deirdre's birth, had come true.

Passed down orally for countless generations, the story of Naoise and Deirdre belongs to the Ulster Cycle of Irish legends, which are believed to be set around the 1st century BC. One of the first written versions appears in the *Book of Leinster*, compiled around AD 1150. Historians' opinions differ as to whether Deirdre, Naoise and his brothers actually existed, but place names around Loch Etive suggest their presence. Old maps show Eilean Uisneachan ('the island of the sons of Uisneach') and Coille Nathais ('Naoise's wood'). On a promontory near the mouth of the loch, overlooking the islands in the Firth of Lorn, is a hill fort anciently known as Dun Mac Uisneachan ('the fort of the sons of Uisneach'); according to tradition, this is where Deirdre and Naoise made their home.

BEN GULABIN

Looming like a guardian over the head of Glen Shee in Highland Perthshire, Ben Gulabin (in Gaelic, *Beinn Ghulbain*) holds the key to one of the most romantic tales in Scottish and Irish legend. At 2,644 feet (806 metres), it is a mere stripling compared to its near neighbours, but this is still wild country: in autumn, red deer stags bellow to their rivals from the high slopes and in winter the snowfields are laced with the footprints of mountain hares.

The story of Diarmuid and Gráinne begins in Ireland with a great warrior-hero called Fionn Mac Cumhaill. As a boy, Fionn had tasted the flesh of the Salmon of Knowledge while cooking it for his druid master, and by doing so he had imbibed all the wisdom of the world. In battle, Fionn and his band of warriors, the Fianna, were invincible, but when it came to choosing a wife he was doomed to heartache and jealousy.

Diarmuid was blessed (or cursed) with a 'love spot' on his forehead, which made every woman fall in love with him.

The woman whom Fionn had pledged to marry was Gráinne, the beautiful daughter of the High King of Ireland. But when Fionn came to the king's seat at Tara for a feast, Gráinne's eyes were drawn instead to a young warrior named Diarmuid O'Duibhne. Diarmuid was blessed (or cursed) with a 'love spot' on his forehead, which made every woman fall in love with him; he usually concealed it beneath a cap, but Gráinne glimpsed it while he was driving apart two snarling dogs and instantly she fell in love with him. She decided that Diarmuid, not Fionn, would be her choice.

To all of the guests except Diarmuid, Gráinne gave a draught of enchanted wine, which sent them into a deep sleep. Then she placed Diarmuid under a 'druid bond', which was an oath constraining him to do her bidding. Together they ran away from the feast, crossing a river to throw Fionn's hounds off their scent and taking shelter in a wood. Soon, though, they knew that Fionn and all of the Fianna were after them and they could never rest for long in one place.

Diarmuid's loyalties were torn. He said to Gráinne: 'I left my own people that were brighter than lime or snow; their heart was full of generosity to me, like the sun that is high above us; but now they follow me angrily, to every harbour and every strand ... O Gráinne, white as snow, it would have been a better choice for you to have given hatred to me, or gentleness to the head of the Fianna.' (Lady Gregory, *Gods and Fighting Men*, 1905.)

But Gráinne was undeterred and she won Diarmuid's heart. They faced many challenges, but eventually found a place of safety across the sea in Alba, far away from Fionn Mac Cumhaill, where they lived to have four sons and a daughter. On two consecutive nights, Diarmuid woke to hear hounds baying; Gráinne persuaded him to stay indoors, but, when it happened again on the third night, Diarmuid went out and followed the noise to the summit of Ben Gulabin. There he found Fionn waiting for him.

Fionn told Diarmuid that a ferocious wild boar – 'the earless Green Boar of Beinn Ghulbain' – had escaped from the huntsmen and was rampaging about the hill. Then Fionn slipped away, knowing that Diarmuid was too courageous to retreat and therefore fated to die. The boar appeared: Diarmuid's loyal hound saw it and fled, but Diarmuid stood firm as it charged. His spears bounced off the animal's hide and his sword broke as he tried to stab it; he caught hold of its neck and clung on as it galloped down the mountain and back up again. Soon he was thrown off and the boar savaged him with its tusks; grievously wounded, Diarmuid struck the creature with his sword and killed it.

Fionn had returned to the scene and was gloating at his rival's downfall; Diarmuid implored him to fetch some healing water from a spring, which would save his life. Fionn grudgingly went to collect some water in his hands, but on the way back he thought of Gráinne and let it spill through his fingers. On his third attempt, he saw that he was too late: Diarmuid had died.

Gráinne's grief was unbearable. 'O Diarmuid,' she cried, 'it is a hard bed Fionn has given you, to be lying on the stones and to be wet with the rain ... your blue eyes to be without sight, you that were friendly and generous and pursuing.' Diarmuid's body was placed on a golden bier and given a hero's burial. Meanwhile Fionn treated Gráinne with gentleness – some said he put a spell on her – and she was persuaded to go away with him. But, in the wider story (or cycle) of which this tale is just one part, Fionn's glory was dwindling.

Ben Gulabin still remembers Diarmuid's fate. Near the summit, a groove between two ridges is called *Leabaidh an Tuirc*, 'the Boar's Bed', and a small loch nearby was described in the late 1800s as *Loch an Tuirc*, 'the Boar's Loch'. A little further down the glen, a mound set with four upright stones is known as Diarmuid's Grave. These stones (now believed to date from the Bronze Age) are said to form the shape of a spearhead, pointing to the place where the boar was killed.

This whole landscape is thick with enchantment. Glen Shee, in Gaelic, is *Gleann Sith* ('the glen of the fairies'), and from high on Ben Gulabin a burn tumbles down from *Coire Shith* ('the fairies' corrie'); perhaps it was from here that Fionn Mac Cumhaill tried so unsuccessfully to fetch healing water.

There are several other locations connected with Diarmuid and Gráinne: in Glen Lonan, Argyll, a standing stone called Diarmuid's Pillar is traditionally believed to mark his grave; across the Irish Sea, the boar hunt was said to have taken place on Ben Bulbin in County Sligo.

GLEN LYON

One of Scotland's most picturesque glens cuts a deep furrow through Highland Perthshire, from Loch Lyon in the west to the village of Fortingall, some 30 miles (48km) to the east. Springing from the high hills that flank it on either side, waterfalls add impetus and volume to the River Lyon, which snakes in generous curves around the valley floor and then crashes noisily through a wooded gorge.

Glen Lyon has long been considered a mysterious place; perhaps this arises partly from its topography, because there is no way out of its westernmost end, except on foot. But there are other factors, too. In the late 1800s, Duncan Campbell, a lifelong resident, revealed that the glen is connected with the legendary Irish hero Fionn Mac Cumhaill and his band of fighting men called the Fianna. Campbell explains: 'A chain of round towers stretches through its whole length, which people still call *Caistealan nam Fiann*, castles of the Fingalians.' Referring to an old name for Glen Lyon, he quotes an old saying: 'Fingal had twelve castles in the crooked glen of large stones.' (*The Lairds of Glenlyon*, 1886.)

Some sources claim that the Fingalians' castles numbered nearer 20, but little remains of them now except a few tumbles of lichen-covered stones. Historically speaking, these may be the remnants of Pictish forts ... but Fionn's presence won't be dismissed so easily. Near Cashlie, in the upper part of the glen, the *Bhacain* or Dog Stake Stone was reputedly where the Fianna tethered their hunting dogs – including the formidable Brân, Fionn's own hound, who was said to be the strongest and most loyal dog that ever lived.

> *Because of its curious appearance, this rock is known as 'the Praying Hands'.*

Fionn himself is said to have fired an arrow and split a large boulder that stands high on the south side of the glen. Because of its curious appearance, this rock is known as 'the Praying Hands'. While their elders sat in solemn council, the younger members of the Fianna indulged in weightlifting contests with rounded boulders, which had to be picked up and placed on a higher stone; one of these, called 'the Testing Stone of the Fianna', still sits in Glen Lyon, presumably where the last competitor dropped it.

But, concealed in the glen, a small man-made shelter, about 16 inches (0.4 metres) high, harbours a secret that may be older even than the stories of the Fianna. Beneath its roof sit two figures, which are actually naturally water-worn stones, called the Bodach ('old man') and the Cailleach ('old woman'). They have a daughter (the Nighean) and a number of smaller children, each represented as pebbles. In a practice that may be the oldest uninterrupted pagan ritual in Britain, the Cailleach and the Bodach are placed outside their house every spring and returned to their shelter every autumn.

This simple act is believed to honour an ancient creator-goddess, also called the Cailleach (from the old Irish *Caillech*, meaning 'veiled one'). Her power and energy were seen in the cycle of life and death, and in the turn of the seasons. Usually depicted as a fearsome one-eyed crone, she could call down the snows and the storms of winter, but in spring she yielded to another goddess, sometimes named as Brigid or Brìghde, who

bestowed fertility and abundance. It has been suggested that these two contrasting figures may be dual aspects of the same deity.

The Cailleach was seen as a protector of animals, and, at a time when cattle were regularly driven up to the high slopes for summer grazing, she was believed to watch over them from her 'house', granting fine weather and good pasture. Often the last sheaf of the harvest was dedicated to her, in the hope of a plentiful crop the following season. Some observers have found a connection between the place name of Glen Lyon and Lugh, a sun-god whose wife was the Cailleach.

Local folklore explains the origin of the shrine. During a snowstorm, a man and his pregnant wife came down from the mountains into Glen Lyon and begged for shelter. The residents offered them a home, in which the woman gave birth to a daughter. It transpired that as long as these newcomers lived in the glen, the land was fertile and the livestock flourished. But one day the family announced their departure. They promised the generous people of Glen Lyon that, as long as their memory was honoured, this prosperity would continue. So three rounded stones were chosen to represent the family and a little house was built for them; every year at Beltane, the festival marking the beginning of summer, they were brought out into the sunlight, and their house was regularly re-roofed in preparation for winter. Occasionally – some say every 100 years – a new stone is added, to symbolise the birth of another child.

History and legend have grown together in Glen Lyon. When plague swept through the glen in the 7th century, it is said that Saint Adomnán, an abbot of Iona Abbey, exorcised the evil spirits that had brought the disease by imprisoning them in a rock. In the churchyard at Fortingall, a huge yew tree, said to be at least 5,000 years old, is linked in folklore with Pontius Pilate, the Roman official who presided over the trial of Christ. It is claimed that Pilate was the son of a local woman and a Roman diplomat who was visiting a Pictish king – that he was born near the tree and was taken to Rome by his father.

SCHIEHALLION

Viewed from the west, across the wild, peaty expanse of Rannoch Moor, the slopes of Schiehallion taper gracefully into an almost perfect conical peak. Perhaps it is this mountain's pleasing symmetry, together with the fact that it sits at the geographical 'heart' of Scotland, that has endowed it with a special significance, and even an aura of magic. To the *Caledonii*, the tribes who occupied the Highlands during the Iron Age, this was *Sith Chailleann,* 'the fairy hill of the Caledonians', and for generations, in turf-roofed bothies and in lairds' halls, they wove all kinds of tales about its spirits and its power.

Highland folklore speaks of a fearsome hag-goddess called the Cailleach Bheur, who ushers in the winter by washing her plaid in the whirlpool of the Corryvreckan (between the islands of Scarba and Jura) and spreading it out to dry on the hills, where it appears as the first snow of winter. Throughout the darkest months, whenever the Cailleach strikes her blackthorn staff on the ground, she summons the frost and the snow. With the onset of spring, however, she turns to stone and is replaced by a goddess in the form of a beautiful maiden, sometimes named as Brigid or Brìghde, whose benevolent influence persists until the following autumn.

Schiehallion has long been believed to be a haunt of the Cailleach, who rode about the mountain during fierce storms, her face blue with cold and her hair encrusted with ice. Travellers who felt the grip of her icy fingers knew that they should quickly seek their firesides or else face certain death.

If the Cailleach failed to seize the unwary hillwalker, he or she might easily stumble into Schiehallion's enchanted cave, inhabited by fairies, from which a dark passage led straight into the Underworld. No one who entered the cave was ever able to return, because a door closed shut behind them. It is little wonder that, every May Day, Schiehallion's human inhabitants would bring offerings of flowers to a natural spring called the Fairy Well on the slopes of the mountain, perhaps in the hope of persuading the fairies – or the Cailleach – to cast a tolerant eye on them.

And it seems that there were quite a few people brave enough to live on Schiehallion, at least for part of the year. Schiehallion's slopes are scattered with the remains of 'shielings' – temporary huts in which people dwelt during the summer, when they moved their cattle to higher pasture. Those months spent on the mountain must have held their own natural magic, with the sun's afterglow lingering on the horizon throughout the night and the calls of nesting birds filling the warm air. But, as the evenings grew cooler and darker, the prospect of autumn storms would send Schiehallion's residents back down to the glens.

In 1899, an ornamented stone cup with the remains of a handle, thought to date back to the Bronze Age, was found close to the summit of Schiehallion. It is tempting to wonder who might have used it, and for what purpose: catching water, perhaps, from one of the springs. Echoing this idea, on a full moon in April 2018, artists Alexander and Susan Maris collected an ounce of water from Schiehallion and carried it on foot to Tobar na h-Aoise, the Well of Eternal Youth on the island of Iona, following old paths that included an ancient coffin route called the Road of the Kings. Their journey, which took them just over two weeks, aimed to explore the relationship between myth and landscape.

It was with a more precise scientific purpose that, in 1774, a group of scientists carrying theodolites, barometers and quadrants trudged up the side of Schiehallion. They were led by Britain's Astronomer Royal, Nevil Maskelyne, and their experiment, funded by the Royal Society, was inspired by theories propounded in the 17th century by Sir Isaac Newton. Quite simply, they hoped to use Schiehallion in order to measure the mass of the entire Earth. Newton believed that every object in the universe, however minuscule, exerts a pull on every other object, meaning that a plumb line suspended close

Travellers who felt the grip of her icy fingers knew that they should quickly seek their firesides or else face certain death.

to a mountain would be pulled very slightly from its vertical position by the mountain's mass.

By measuring this deviation on either side of Schiehallion, and doing some mind-boggling mathematics, Maskelyne and his surveyor, Charles Hutton, calculated the density and, by extrapolation, the mass of the Earth with a respectable degree of accuracy. Hutton's mapping work involved 'the connecting together by a faint line all the points which were of the same relative altitude'. (C. Hutton, *An Account of the Calculations made from the Survey and Measures taken at Schehallien*, Royal Society of London, 1778.) For this reason, he is now considered to be the inventor of contour lines.

After several miserably wet months in their small purpose-built bothy, Maskelyne and his team invited some local people to a party, which was so merry that the building caught fire and burned to the ground. Luckily no one was harmed, and Maskelyne reputedly replaced the fiddler's lost violin with a Stradivarius!

Folk singer Iona Lane invoked the extraordinary scene in her song 'Schiehallion':

> Long into the night
> A local fiddler's tune ignites
> Alone in the sky
> We toast Schiehallion goodbye

(Iona Lane, 'Schiehallion', 2022)

BEN MACDUI

Ben Macdui (in Gaelic, *Beinn Mac Duibh*, possibly meaning 'Macduff's mountain') is the second-highest mountain in Scotland and in Britain, rising to 4,295 feet (1,309 metres). Ascending it from any direction involves a long and arduous walk over rough terrain, and the notoriously changeable weather of the Cairngorm plateau means that climbers must be prepared for ferocious conditions at any time of year. From the summit cairn, a vast panorama of mountains and small lochs sweeps away in all directions. But while they are pausing to rest after their exertion, some walkers have sensed a mysterious and unwelcome companion.

Speaking at the annual dinner of The Cairngorm Club in November 1925, the Honorary President, Norman J. Collie, made a startling revelation. In misty weather, with snow underfoot, he had climbed alone to the summit of Ben Macdui and was beginning the descent when he distinctly heard the sound of footsteps crunching on the snow behind him. From their frequency, it seemed that whoever was following him was taking strides three or four times the length of his own.

Seeing nothing through the mist, Collie continued on his way. But he could still hear footsteps close behind and suddenly he was seized with terror. He took to his heels and ran, stopping only when he was close to the Rothiemurchus Forest some four or five miles (6.5–8km) away.

A professor of Chemistry and a fellow of the Royal Society, Collie was one of the most respected mountaineers of his generation, having climbed in the Himalayas, the Alps and the Rockies as well as the Scottish Highlands. He was accustomed to being on his own in the mountains, and was not given to flights of imagination, but he concluded his talk by saying that he would never go back to Ben Macdui alone.

Collie's announcement caused a sensation, but he was not the only person to have experienced weird things on Ben Macdui. In the late 1800s two seasoned climbers, Alexander and Henry Kellas, were collecting mineral specimens on a slope below the summit. They glanced up to see a giant figure coming towards them. It passed out of sight into a fold of the hill, but before it could reappear on the side nearest to them they were gripped by an unnatural fear and fled.

When this story was recounted to a man from Rothiemurchus, who was familiar with the Cairngorms, he knew exactly what it was. 'That,' he said, 'would have been the *Fear Liath Mòr*.'

The *Fear Liath Mòr*, or 'Big Grey Man' of Ben Macdui, seems to be adept at spooking the toughest and most pragmatic of climbers. In 1946 a leader of the Cairngorms RAF Rescue Team felt a sinister 'presence', heard mysterious footsteps and was overcome by such dread that he found himself running headlong towards the precipice known as Lurcher's Crag. He tried to swerve away from this disastrous course and succeeded only with great difficulty. Another intrepid camper on the summit reported seeing a gigantic figure blotting out the moonlight that streamed into his tent, and then watched as it moved away down the hill; he estimated that it was 20 feet (6 metres) tall.

Over the decades, the unsettling sights and sounds of Ben

Macdui have been so numerous that some people have sought to explain them with science. Theories have been put forward to explain the footsteps, including the audible cracking of deep snow which has been lying for some time, and streams flowing noisily beneath the surface of a scree slope. However, the sound has also been heard in dry summer weather. As for the apparitions, a natural atmospheric phenomenon known as a Brocken spectre is occasionally seen from high vantage points: named after a mountain in Germany, this occurs when observers see their own enormous shadow projected by the sun onto low cloud amid a circular halo of brilliant light.

These explanations sound plausible but they don't account for the disembodied voices, music and ringing sounds that have also been heard on and around Ben Macdui. In 1970 the writer Affleck Grey, who grew up in the Cairngorms, published a collection of accounts from a wide range of sources, including one of his own. However, as a lifelong hillwalker, he remained convinced that no harm would ever befall him in the mountains.

Another intrepid camper on the summit reported seeing a gigantic figure blotting out the moonlight that streamed into his tent.

In his book *Celtic Sacred Landscapes* (1996) Nigel Pennick explains that, in early cultures, mountains and other features in the landscape were perceived as being inhabited by spirits – *anima loci* – which possessed their own consciousness and personality, and could be sensed as a feeling or an atmosphere. He suggests that, by our own awareness and actions, we bring these unseen spirits into physical presence. This concept, or some form of it, has been considered by several witnesses to Ben Macdui's eerie phenomena.

Despite its reputation as Scotland's haunted mountain, Ben Macdui holds a special place in the hearts of hillwalkers. For the climber and writer Cameron McNeish, it is the one Cairngorm summit he never tires of visiting: in his book *Come by the Hills* (2020) he reveals how much he loves the spaciousness, the vast open skies and the breathtaking views that can reach as far as Caithness in the north and the Lammermuirs in the south.

In 1925, when The Cairngorm Club installed a custom-made indicator at the summit, pointing to recognisable landmarks in all directions, an enthusiastic crowd of 140 men, women and children attended the unveiling ceremony. Describing the extraordinary turnout in its journal, The Cairngorm Club concluded with a sentiment that might give the Big Grey Man pause for thought:

> Our newly-born indicator, brought to life amid such happy auguries, was indeed to be 'sleeping out and far to-night', but perchance the benign Spirit of the Mountain administered that solace which is never denied to those who seek her inner shrine.

(Robert Clarke, *The Cairngorm Club Journal*, July 1926)

ISLE OF STAFFA

While touring Scotland in 1829, the composer Felix Mendelssohn wrote to his sister, Fanny: 'In order to make you understand how extraordinarily the Hebrides affected me, I send you the following, which came into my head there.'

He then jotted down the opening bars of a piece of music inspired by a jaw-dropping natural wonder: the towering cliffs and dark caves of a Hebridean island known as Staffa. The composition was completed in 1830 and published three years later; originally entitled 'The Hebrides Overture', it is more familiarly known as 'Fingal's Cave'.

The geological gem that is Staffa lies about 6 miles (10km) west of the Isle of Mull; it has a surface area of only 82 acres (33 hectares) and rises to 138 feet (42 metres). Its extraordinary appearance is the result of volcanic activity some 59 million years ago, when lava flows cooled very slowly to form spectacular vertical columns of black basalt. These are topped with a thick layer of amorphous basalt, which has a scrambled texture, and the result is reminiscent of a gigantic soufflé that has risen out of its dish and is in danger of collapsing over the sides.

Early Norse voyagers were convinced that Staffa was built by the gods. Its name comes from the Old Norse *stafi-oy*, meaning 'stave-' or 'pillar-island', possibly because the Norsemen were reminded of the vertical wooden staves that they used for building. However, for many centuries its remote location meant that few outsiders ever got to see it, and it was only in August 1772, when the botanist Sir Joseph Banks stopped

there on his way to Iceland, that it attracted the attention of scientists.

Banks ventured into a magnificent sea-washed cave whose straight sides rise up to a 'roof' resembling a vaulted ceiling. His guide informed him that this was the Cave of Fiuhn or Fingal, named after the warrior-hero of Irish legend, Fionn Mac Cumhaill. Banks noted this name in his journal, and thereafter it was always referred to as Fingal's Cave; however, the Gaelic place name *Uamh Bhin* actually means 'the melodious cave', invoking the musical resonance of the waves breaking within it. Banks's guide may have supplied him with a more mythical alternative!

Banks had sailed around the world with Captain James Cook, but he had never seen anything quite like Staffa. He wrote: 'Compared to this, what are the cathedrals or the palaces built by man – mere models or playthings, imitations as diminutive as his works will always be when compared to those of nature ....' (*Journal of a Voyage up Great Britain's West Coast and to Iceland*, 1772.) He observed that Staffa's geology strongly resembled that of the Giant's Causeway in Northern Ireland (which is comprised of similar basalt columns) and speculated about their connection. It is now known that these two formations resulted from volcanic activity of a similar age, although the lavas came from different volcanoes.

After Banks's rapt descriptions were made public, boatloads of intrepid visitors braved the rough sea-crossing to Staffa, eager to be astonished. Among them were Queen Victoria and Prince Albert, the artist J.M.W. Turner, and the writers Jules Verne, Sir Walter Scott and Robert Louis Stevenson. Feeding the Victorians' hunger for romance, Staffa's folklore was revived (or perhaps reinvented): it was said to be a stepping stone from Ireland to Scotland, thrown by Fionn Mac Cumhaill who strode across the Irish Sea from the Giant's Causeway to fight his Scottish counterpart, a giant called Benandonner.

Staffa looks an inhospitable place to live at the best of times, but archaeologists at the National Trust for Scotland have proved that it was occupied – or at least visited – during the Bronze Age. Burnt grains of barley, found within the traces of a structure, have been dated to between 1880 and 1700 BC. Future investigations hope to determine whether this occupation was domestic or ritualistic.

In his book *The Scottish Islands* (1996), Hamish Haswell-Smith records that in 1772, the time of Joseph Banks's visit, Staffa had a population of one; by 1784 it had risen to 16, and the residents were somehow managing to scratch enough soil to grow barley, oats, flax and potatoes. By 1800, however, the island had been abandoned by humans, leaving behind only the puffins and guillemots that nest every summer on its grass-topped cliffs.

Fingal's Cave is a natural amplifier of sound, and in the 19th century Archibald MacArthur, piper to Ranald MacDonald of Staffa, would often stand at the mouth of the cave and play a *pibroch* or traditional air on the bagpipes to welcome visitors in true Highland fashion. In more recent years, musicians have brought flutes, cellos, guitars or simply their own voices into the flooded chamber, allowing their music to mingle with the rhythmic swell and sigh of the sea.

CALANAIS

A voice so thrilling ne'er was heard
In spring-time from the Cuckoo-bird,
Breaking the silence of the seas
Among the farthest Hebrides.

(William Wordsworth, 'The Solitary Reaper' from
Poems, in Two Volumes, 1807)

At first sight, it is the rawness of the stones that strikes you, as they heave themselves up from the earth and punctuate the vast Hebridean sky like the teeth of some half-buried monster. Their size is formidable – the central pillar is well over 15 feet (4.5 metres) high – but at close range the shaded bands of Lewisian gneiss swirl and ripple across their faces, with here and there a nugget of white quartz and a crusting of bronze lichen.

For 5,000 years they have been standing here, on a windswept ridge overlooking Loch Roag on the Isle of Lewis. Seen from above, they form the shape of a cross, with three short 'arms' radiating south, east and west from a slightly flattened circle some 42 feet (13 metres) across, and a double row of stones extending for 90 yards (82 metres) to the north; walking down this majestic avenue towards the central ring, it is impossible to resist wondering who, or what, might have passed along it before.

According to local folklore, every year at sunrise on the summer solstice, something known as 'the shining one' would walk down this great avenue towards the circle, heralded by the cuckoo's call. This story was known to local crofters in the early 19th century, and could well be a very ancient memory. It has been conjectured that Calanais was constructed as an astronomical observatory, and that 'the shining one' refers to the planet Venus, which often appears as a morning star. The cuckoo, which was one of the sacred birds of the Hebrides, may have represented fertility.

In Gaelic, the stones are known as the *Fir Bhreig* or 'false men', perhaps alluding to their appearance from a distance. A centuries-old tale, which is echoed (with variations) at many other stone circles, is that they were originally giants who refused to build a

church and were turned to stone by way of punishment. But another story, which has a sense of something much older, tells how a white cow appeared out of the sea during a time of famine and spoke softly to a local woman, telling her to bring her neighbours to the stone circle. Every day the cow yielded full pails of milk for the starving people, but when a witch appeared with a pierced bucket and milked the cow dry, the animal disappeared and was never seen again.

From Calanais it is possible to see the southern hills of Lewis, whose profile is said to resemble a sleeping woman (in Gaelic, *Cailleach na Mointeach*, 'the old woman of the moors'). Every 18.6 years, the moon appears to skim the hills, travelling along the woman's 'body' and dropping down behind her head. It has been suggested that this phenomenon, combined

> *Every year at sunrise on the summer solstice, something known as 'the shining one' would walk down this great avenue towards the circle.*

with the *Cailleach* place name, harks back to a time when an Earth-goddess was seen to bestow fertility and abundance, restoring light and life to the landscape.

The stones themselves have not always been as exposed as they are today. It is believed that from about 1000 BC they were choked by a gradual build-up of peat, which was removed during an excavation in 1857. However, there was enough visible in the late 1600s for the Scottish writer Martin Martin to inspect the site and make enquiries among local residents. He was told that Calanais had been a place of heathen worship, when the chief druid would stand near the tallest stone and address himself to the people. In the 19th century the old tradition of visiting the stones on May Day and Midsummer's Day was still being observed, despite the disapproval of church ministers.

It is believed that Calanais was the focus of ritual activity for over a thousand years after it was built. In a small chambered cairn beneath the tallest stone, traces of cremated human bone have been found. Nearby, over a dozen more stone circles or individual standing stones have been identified, smaller in scale but just as enigmatic, indicating that this windswept landscape held a special place in Neolithic and Bronze Age culture. In 2020 it was revealed that a lightning strike had taken place in the exact centre of a stone circle known as Calanais XI, and archaeologists are now investigating whether the strike happened before or after the circle was built – in other words, whether the stones were placed there to mark the event.

SELECTED BIBLIOGRAPHY

Armistead, Wilson, *Tales and Legends of the English Lakes* (Simpkin, Marshall & Co, 1891)

Ashe, Geoffrey, *Mythology of the British Isles* (Guild, 1990)

Aubrey, John, *Monumenta Britannica* (c. 1663–93)

Barber, Chris, *Mysterious Wales* (David & Charles, 1982)

Baring-Gould, Sabine, *The Book of the West* (Methuen, 1900)

Berresford Ellis, Peter, *A Dictionary of Irish Mythology* (Constable, 1987)

Bray, Anna Eliza, *Traditions, Legends, Superstitions and Sketches of Devonshire* (John Murray, 1838)

Burl, Aubrey, *The Stone Circles of the British Isles* (Yale University, 1976)

Burne, Charlotte Sophia, *The Handbook of Folklore* (Folklore Society, 1914)

Campbell, John Gregorson, *Superstitions of the Highlands & Islands of Scotland* (James MacLehose & Sons, 1900)

Courtney, M.A., *Cornish Feasts and Folk-lore* (Beare and Son, 1890)

Crane, Nicholas, *The Making of the British Landscape* (Weidenfeld & Nicolson, 2016)

Delaney, Frank, *The Legends of the Celts* (Hodder & Stoughton, 1989)

Ebbutt, M.I. (ed. John Matthews), *Hero Myths & Legends of Britain & Ireland* (Blandford, 1995)

Gregory, Lady, *Gods and Fighting Men* (John Murray, 1905)

Guest, Edwin, *Origines Celticae* (Macmillan & Co, 1883)

Guest, Lady Charlotte, *The Mabinogion* (J.M. Dent & Co, 1906)

Henderson, William, *Notes on the Folk-lore of the Northern Counties of England and the Borders* (W. Satchell, Peyton & Co, 1879)

Holinshed, Raphael, *Chronicles of England, Scotland and Ireland* (1577)

Hutchinson, William, *The History of the County of Cumberland* (F. Jollie, 1794)

Kingshill, Sophia and Jennifer Westwood, *The Fabled Coast* (Random House, 2012)

Macfarlane, Robert, *The Old Ways* (Hamish Hamilton, 2012)

Malory, Sir Thomas, *Le Morte d'Arthur* (c. 1485)

Martin, Martin, *A Description of the Western Islands of Scotland* (1703)

Matthews, John and Caitlin, *British & Irish Mythology* (Aquarian Press, 1988)

Monmouth, Geoffrey of, *Historia regum Britanniae* (c. 1136)

Ochota, Mary-Ann, *Hidden Histories* (Frances Lincoln, 2016)

Ochota, Mary-Ann, *Secret Britain* (Frances Lincoln, 2020)

Pennant, Thomas, *A Tour in Wales* (Henry Hughes, 1778)

Rackham, Oliver, *The History of the Countryside* (Phoenix, 1986)

Rackham, Oliver, *Trees & Woodland in the British Landscape* (J.M. Dent, 1976)

Radford, E. & M.A. (ed. Christina Hole), *The Encyclopedia of Superstitions* (Hutchinson & Co, 1980)

Ross, Anne, *The Folklore of the Scottish Highlands* (Batsford, 1976)

Smith, Reginald Bosworth, *Bird Life and Bird Lore* (John Murray, 1905)

Squire, Charles, *The Mythology of the British Islands* (Blackie, 1905)

Straffon, Cheryl, *The Earth Goddess: Celtic and Pagan Legacy of the Landscape* (Blandford, 1997)

Trevelyan, Marie, *Folk-lore and Folk-stories of Wales* (Elliot Stock, 1909)

Westwood, Jennifer, *Albion: A Guide to Legendary Britain* (Granada, 1985)

Westwood, Jennifer and Jacqueline Simpson, *The Lore of the Land* (Penguin, 2005)

Wood, Michael, *In Search of the Dark Ages* (BBC, 1981)

Wood, Michael, *In Search of England* (Viking, 1999)

Also:

Folklore, the journal of The Folklore Society

Scottish Geographical Magazine

Websites and online records of: National Trust, English Heritage, CADW, Coflein (National Monuments Record of Wales), Historic Environment Scotland, Canmore (Scotland's National Record of Historic Environment), National Trust for Scotland.

INDEX

ACKNOWLEDGEMENTS

I owe a huge debt of gratitude to many people who have helped to shape this book, from the first spark of an idea right through to the beautifully crafted, finished version.

Firstly, I'd like to acknowledge the writers, folklorists and storytellers who continue to celebrate Britain's landscape in so many ways. Without their talents and passion, a treasure-trove of folklore and legend would be lost.

Thank you to the following writers, poets and songwriters (or their publishers) for giving kind permission to reproduce quotes and lyrics: page 2: Philip Marsden, *The Summer Isles* (Granta, 2019); page 50: J.R.R. Tolkien, *The Two Towers*, reprinted by permission of HarperCollins Publishers Ltd © 1954; page 123: Alan Garner, *The Weirdstone of Brisingamen*, reprinted by permission of HarperCollins Publishers Ltd © 1960; page 170: 'Enlli' by Christine Evans: *Selected Poems* (Seren, 2003); page 202: Iona Lane, 'Schiehallion', 2022.

To Joe Mason, my grateful thanks for sharing information about the Great Stone of Lyng.

To Verity Rimmer, editor at the National Trust, thank you for liaising so efficiently with the team of archaeologists who are responsible for the National Trust sites included here, and for being so helpful with the text.

To the team of National Trust archaeologists and staff at properties, thank you so much for giving your time to share your knowledge about these amazing places and for casting an expert eye over the relevant chapters. In particular, I'd like to thank Martin Papworth, Angus Wainwright, Laura Howarth, Russell Clement, Gillian Mason, Adrian Cox, Michael Clarke, Jamie Lund, Paul Farrington, Georgia Fitzpatrick, Kate Picker, Mark Newman, Nick Snashall, Janet Tomlin, Philippa Puzey-Broomhead, James Gould, Simon Rogers, Virginia Portman, Steven Michell and Shannon Hogan.

To Claire Harrup, thank you for the gorgeous illustrations – to me, they seem to capture the quality of other-worldliness that makes these landscapes so special.

At HarperCollins, a very big thank you to David Salmo and Peter Taylor for your enthusiasm and support – as always, it was a pleasure to work with you. Thank you also to Gill Knappett for meticulous copy-editing.

To my friends at the Royal Scottish Geographical Society, thank you for being so supportive of everything that I do; and likewise thank you to the readers of my blog, The Hazel Tree – it is wonderful to know how many people revere and appreciate these places, where you can almost feel the legends beneath your feet.

And to my family – Colin, Verity and Leonie – endless love and thanks. This is for you.